THE SEARCH AND SEIZURE HANDBOOK
FOR LAW OFFICERS

THIRD (REVISED) EDITION

by Devallis Rutledge

CUSTOM PUBLISHING COMPANY

CUSTOM PUBLISHING COMPANY

1590 Lotus Road
Placerville, California 95667
(916) 626-1260

Your Partner in Education
with
"QUALITY TEXTS AT FAIR PRICES"

The
Search and Seizure Handbook
For Law Officers

Third (Revised) Edition

Copyright 1989 by Custom Publishing Company

Developmental Editor - Derald Hunt

All rights reserved. No portion of this book may be reprinted or reproduced in any manner without prior written permission of the publisher; except for brief passages which may be quoted in connection with a book review and only when source credit is given.

Library of Congress Catalog Number 84-72123

ISBN 0-942728-39-4 Paper Text Edition

Printed in the United States of America.

THE SEARCH AND SEIZURE HANDBOOK
FOR LAW OFFICERS

THIRD (REVISED) EDITION

About the Author...

Devallis Rutledge is also the author of:

The Officer Survival Manual, The New Police Report Manual, and Courtroom Survival: The Officer's Guide to Better Testimony.

His Books are widely used by law enforcement agencies and colleges in all 50 states and several foreign countries. Rutledge is a former veteran police officer and current Prosecuting Attorney. He has taught law enforcement subjects to hundreds of students and officers of more than 50 police, sheriff's, highway patrol departments and colleges.

The Search & Seizure Handbook, like all of his other books, is written for the field officer and student in clear, straightforward language, with scores of examples taken from real-life field situations.

CUSTOM PUBLISHING COMPANY

DEDICATION

Dedicated to the nation's peace officers and to those who are studying to prepare themselves for the challenging and rewarding field of professional law enforcement.

Devallis Rutledge

CONTENTS

Chapter   Page

PART ONE
THE SEARCH AND SEIZURE PROBLEM

1   NEED TO KNOW 13
      Effect of the exclusionary rule and federal civil rights laws on law enforcement activities.

2   DISASSEMBLY OF THE 4th AMENDMENT .. 23
      Step-by-step analysis of the key words and phrases in the 4th Amendment.

PART TWO
SEARCH AND SEIZURE WITHOUT A WARRANT

3   NO REASONABLE EXPECTATION
     OF PRIVACY 41
       Plain View *43*
       Abandoned Property *46*
       No Standing *49*
       Open Fields *51*
       Public Places *53*
       Jail Searches *57*
       Eavesdropping *59*
       Phone Monitors *61*
       Pen Registers *62*
       Wires *64*
       Optical Aids *65*
       Beepers........................ *68*
       Ruse And Trick *69*

4 SEARCH WARRANT EXCEPTIONS 75
- *Probable Cause* 76
- *One Step at a Time* 79
- *Scope of Search* 83
- *Emergency* 84
- *Officer Protection* 92
- *Stop and Frisk* 96
- *Carstops: Fleeting Targets* 98
- *Incident to Arrest* 105
- *Hot Pursuit* 111
- *Destruction of Evidence* 116
- *Border Inspections* 120
- *Parole & Probation Searches* 121
- *Consent* 123
- *Private Searches* 128
- *Sample Consent Form* 129
- *Pretext to Search* 133

PART THREE
THE SEARCH WARRANT

5 GETTING THE WARRANT 141
- *What Is a Search Warrant?* 143
- *Objects of a Warrant* 143
- *Form of the Warrant* 144
- *Oath or Affirmation* 145
- *Contents of the Affidavit* 147
- *Describing the Place* 148
- *Describing the Property* 152
- *Officer Expertise* 154

PC for the Search *155*
Seizing Obscene Material *159*
Nighttime Search *160*
Protecting Informants *160*
Photos and Diagrams *161*
Containers *161*
Multiple Targets *162*
Words and Phrases *163*
Conclusion of the Affidavit *163*
Sample Search Warrant *165*
Sample Affidavit *167*

6 SERVING THE WARRANT **173**
Who Can Serve It? *174*
Jurisdiction *174*
Time Limits *176*
Entry *177*
Scope of Search *180*
After the Search *185*
Return of the Warrant *185*

PART FOUR
SAVING THE CASE

7 SALVAGING THE SEARCH AND SEIZURE **189**
Multiple Bases for Searching *190*
Good Faith *195*
Attenuated Taint *196*
Independent Source *198*
Inevitable Discovery *200*

8 WRITING YOUR REPORT 203
Subjective Reporting 204
Search and Seizure Checklist 214

9 THE SUPPRESSION HEARING 221
Burden of Proof 222
Unique Features 222
Your Hardest Job 225
Doing Your Best 233

PART ONE

THE SEARCH AND SEIZURE PROBLEM

Recent Court Decisions

In *Michigan v. Chestnut*, The United States Supreme Court ruled that no Fourth Amendment "detention" had occurred where a marked police car followed a running narcotics suspect around the corner and accelerated alongside him. When the suspect tossed drugs onto the ground, his resulting arrest was valid.

The high court has now ruled, in *California v. Greenwood,* that there is no expectation of privacy in trash that has been put out for collection. Police officers who searched through a suspect's discarded trash could use the evidence of drug transaction they found to obtain a search warrant for the suspect's home.

In *Murray v. U.S.,* the Supreme Court held that evidence seen inside a building, when police legally entered, could later be lawfully seized where officers had already started the process of obtaining a search warrant and eventually "re-discovered" the same evidence during service of the search warrant.

1

NEED TO KNOW

If you saw the Clint Eastwood movie, *Dirty Harry*, you probably remember the scene where Harry was called to the DA's office after capturing the sadistic San Francisco sniper. Harry went in feeling good about his detective work and told the DA: "I got lucky." But the DA wasn't passing out compliments—he angrily accused Harry of violating the sniper's Constitutional rights, said Harry was lucky not to get prosecuted himself, and blamed Harry's poor police procedure for the fact that an obviously-guilty murderer would have to be cut loose.

That movie, and that scene in particular, illustrated the topsy-turvy situation created by modern rules of search and seizure, under which the prosecutors and the courts will inquire into the suspect's guilt or innocence of violating the law *only after* they have inquired into the *officer's* guilt or innocence of violating the suspect's rights. If the procedures followed by the officer in searching for and seizing evidence don't comply with Constitutional, statutory and judicial guidelines, the evidence will be lost, and the criminal may go free.

This uniquely-American state of affairs has been brought about by a judicially-created concept known as "the exclusionary rule." Since 1914 in the federal courts, and since 1961 in all of the state courts, evidence collected by a governmental officer in violation of the 4th Amendment has been subject to being excluded from the criminal trial of the person whose rights were violated. (The exclusionary rule also applies to violations of a suspect's 5th, 6th and 14th Amendment rights.)

The court-given rationale for using the exclusionary rule—which invariably tends to help the criminal get away with his crime—is that by suppressing evidence which an officer had no right to seize, the court will *punish* the officer for violating the Constitution and will *deter* him from making the same mistake again. (Although there is widespread discontent with both this theory and its consequences, the exclusionary rule remains a firmly-entrenched principle of criminal law with which you must be prepared to contend.)

The exclusionary rule applies to all forms of evidence—including an officer's observations. And under the "fruit of the poisonous tree" doctrine, the exclusionary rule extends to any evidence which was directly or indirectly obtained as a result of the initial unlawful search or seizure.

The device the court uses to determine whether or not you violated a suspect's 4th Amendment rights, and whether some or all of the evidence will be excluded (or "suppressed"), is the *suppression hearing*. Whenever the suspect's lawyer feels there is a chance of getting some of the evidence excluded, he will file a motion to suppress the evidence; a court hearing by the judge (no jury) will be scheduled before the trial date. If the judge finds that any of the evidence in the case resulted from an unreasonable search or seizure, he will order it suppressed. Then, if the prosecutor decides that there isn't enough admissible evidence left to warrant a trial, the case may be plea-bargained to a reduced charge or penalty, or it may be dismissed. (Thorough discussion of your role in the suppression hearing is in Chapter 9.)

A large percentage of the cases that get busted down or dismissed because of search-and-seizure errors involve narcotics, weapons, and stolen property crimes. However, the exclusionary rule also often comes into play in such crimes as auto theft, burglary, armed robbery, rape, child molesting, kidnaping and murder. So your failure to learn and abide by the various search-and-seizure rules could mean that a crook gets away with anything from possession of a joint to the murder of a fellow police officer. (Just imagine how you'd feel if a cop-killer got off easy because you never bothered to learn the rules of search and seizure—that thought alone should be enough to motivate you to master search-and-seizure law.)

But the loss of evidence and the loss of a case aren't the only bad consequences of an officer's error in search and seizure. The officer may be prosecuted by the US Department of Justice for depriving the criminal of his civil rights. The officer may be sued by the criminal in federal district court (I've read of jury awards against officers of up to $250,000 for unlawful searches and seizures)—this means that you may be laying your house, your car and your savings account on the line whenever you engage in questionable search-and-seizure activities.

An officer's employer, including supervisors and commanders, the department, and the city, county, state or federal government, may also be sued for failing to properly train and supervise the errant officer. Too many of these lawsuits may result in the loss of liability insurance by the employing agency, which could mean financial disaster in the event of another big lawsuit, especially for smaller departments, cities and counties.

In extreme cases, search-and-seizure violations could result in the cut-off of state or federal law enforcement assistance funds. And, of course, there's all the negative publicity that accompanies these other negative consequences, and bad publicity can lead in turn to demands for civilian review boards.

See all the problems you can cause by following improper procedure for search and seizure? And you

NEED TO KNOW/17

"YOU BLEW IT!"

A reprimand from your supervisor is just one of the problems you can create for yourself by failing to follow proper search and seizure procedures.

can bet that anytime your error results in any of these problems, the very *least* that will happen to you is an uncomfortable series of reprimands—from the judge, the prosecutor, and your superior officers.

And by the very nature of your work, you're going to bump into search-and-seizure issues every time you turn around: can you stop that car? Can you frisk the driver? Can you search him? Can you search his car? The glove compartment? The trunk? The tool box? Can you enter that house? Can you search inside? Can you seize visible evidence and contraband once you get inside? Do you need a search warrant? Can you get a search warrant? Can you seize things that aren't listed in the warrant? Can you eavesdrop? Use binoculars? Tap a phone? Plant a beeper?

As you can see, if you didn't already know it, you simply can't be involved in law enforcement work and not confront search-and-seizure issues practically every day. Virtually every vehicle stop—from traffic citation to drunk driver to fleeing felon—presents the potential for a search-and-seizure issue. Most entries into private houses and other structures raise similar issues. So does the "stop-and-frisk" field detention or interview. For all these reasons, you need to know the law of search and seizure if you're going to be a proficient law enforcement officer.

There was a time when law enforcement was simpler, of course. In those days, an officer was free to follow his nose—he could sniff out crime and criminals on the basis of his street savvy, and if his police instincts turned up evidence, that evidence could be used to convict the criminal. What's more, the evidence was convincing proof that the officer's instincts had been right.

You and I and anyone else who has ever sat behind the wheel of a patrol car for a few months know that there *is* such a thing as street savvy, and we know that an officer's instincts are *right* far more often than they are wrong. Any cop worth his salt can take one look at a pedestrian and know whether the guy needs talking to, or can pick out the cars on the street that are likely to yield weapons or dope or stolen property.

But very few judges or legislators have ever sat behind the wheel of a patrol car. Very few of them have worn a badge down into the rough part of town. Very few of them have spent time talking to people on the street—learning to tell when they're being lied to, learning to smell street dangers, learning to see nervousness and anxiety and other signs of guilt in the way a crook looks at you, or talks to you, or taps his fingers, or jerks his head, or sniffs his nose, or pats his foot, or keeps glancing over at the jacket lying on the car seat. Very few judges or legislators have ever *acquired* street savvy, so very few of them are willing to *recognize* that it exists.

Instead of leaving you on your own to do your police work as only an experienced cop knows how, therefore, the courts and the lawmakers have established a body of rules, liberally derived from the 4th Amendment, to govern your conduct in the area of searches and seizures. Because the concept underlying these rules is not necessarily based on a realistic understanding of criminal behavior and police skill, search-and-seizure law is the most confused and unsettled area of criminal law and procedure. The rules vary greatly from jurisdiction to jurisdiction, and the high rate of appellate reversals of lower court decisions on search-and-seizure issues demonstrates that not even the judges themselves can agree very often on the proper application of 4th Amendment law.

The underlying concept of the rules is that officers who are "engaged in the competitive business of ferreting out crime" cannot always be trusted to observe reasonable restraints in their search-and-seizure activities, but require the supervision of "detached, neutral magistrates" to determine whether or not there is probable cause to conduct a search or seizure. Because, as a practical matter, these "detached, neutral magistrates" lack the street sense to fully appreciate the realities of crime investigation, and because real-life situations often make it impractical or impossible for an officer to get prior approval for his actions from a magistrate, a complicated set of exceptions has been created to try to square the theoretical concept with the facts of life.

For you, the working officer, this means it is essential to understand the basic aspects of search-and-seizure law, to know what your authority and limitations are, to recognize and be able to take full advantage of the established exceptions to the limitations, to become adept at obtaining and serving search warrants when necessary, to become proficient at explaining and justifying (in your report and your testimony) your

NEED TO KNOW/21

search-and-seizure activities, and to help educate prosecutors and judges to the practical considerations of police work, so that the rules governing your work may become more realistic.

Because there is such widespread variation in search-and-seizure rules, no book on the subject could possibly be 100% complete and 100% correct for all jurisdictions. Even within a single state or judicial district, the prevailing rules may be 180 degrees apart in different courts. Therefore, you should view the discussion of search-and-seizure law in this book as *the generally-accepted body of rules,* but with the understanding that local statutes or judicial decisions may create additional guidelines for your department in some areas. I've left spaces throughout the book for you to write in any local modifications for your particular jurisdiction. If you have a question about any given topic or rule, be sure to consult with your supervisor, your prosecuting attorney, a local judge, or your department's legal advisor, and note any local variations in the appropriate space in this book.

Since the law on search and seizure is the fastest-changing in all of criminal law, you should try to keep current in this area with appropriate periodicals, such as *THE LAW OFFICER'S BULLETIN* (published biweekly by the Bureau of National Affairs, Washington, DC), the *SEARCH AND SEIZURE LAW REPORT* (published monthly by Clark Boardman Company, New York), or the *SEARCH AND SEIZURE BULLETIN* (published biweekly by Quinlan Publishing Company, Boston). Many law enforcement magazines also feature regular updates on search-and-seizure issues.

The more you know about the vital law of search and seizure, the less likely you are to make a mistake that could be costly to you personally, to your department, and to the successful prosecution of your cases. Vital information is usually released on a "need-to-know" basis, and every man or woman who wears a badge—regardless of rank or assignment—needs to know the vital information on search and seizure that's in this handbook. It can help you avoid getting yourself into the kind of trouble that not even Dirty Harry could shoot his way out of. ☐

2

DISASSEMBLY OF THE 4TH AMENDMENT

One of the most important topics in academy instruction is use, operation and maintenance of service firearms. Any fool can pick up a gun, point it, and pull the trigger. But not everyone knows what to do if the trigger won't pull because one or more safetys are on. And not everyone knows what to do if the trigger pulls and the hammer drops but nothing happens because the firing pin is broken or missing. Not everyone knows what to do if an automatic jams or the cylinder of a revolver won't turn. Not everyone knows what to do with a misfire. Not everyone knows about things like muzzle velocity, recoil and effective range.

But anyone who's going to carry a firearm in the performance of his duties and depend on that firearm to keep him alive has to know all of these things, and more. That's why you've been trained to disassemble your service weapon and find out "what makes it tick." Once you've learned how all the components fit together and interact with each other, and once you've learned the weapon's capabilities and limitations, you're going to be far more comfortable with the weapon and much more adept at preventing and correcting possible malfunctions.

It's the same with the 4th Amendment, or any other provision of law. If you take it apart and see what makes it tick, you'll understand its operation and its limitations much better. You'll feel far more comfortable with it, and you'll become much more adept at preventing possible violations of it.

Any fool can tell you that the 4th Amendment forbids unreasonable searches and seizures. But not everyone can tell you when the 4th Amendment applies, and when it doesn't. Not everyone can tell you what makes a search or seizure "unreasonable," or what could have been done differently to make it *reasonable.* Not everyone can tell you when you need a search warrant, and when you can get by without one. Not everyone can tell you what it takes to *get* a search warrant, and what you may and may not do in serving it.

We've already established your need to know all of these things. And it isn't enough just to memorize the list of rules and exceptions in a field of law that is

THE 4th AMENDMENT/25

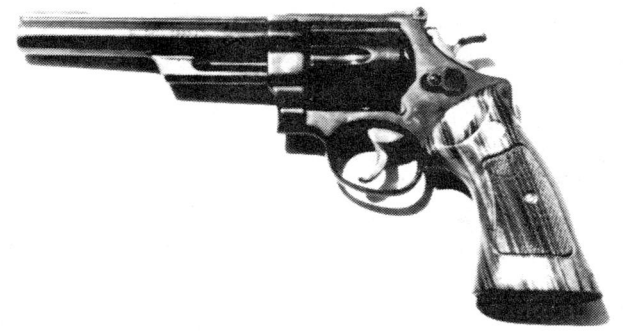

HOW DOES IT WORK?

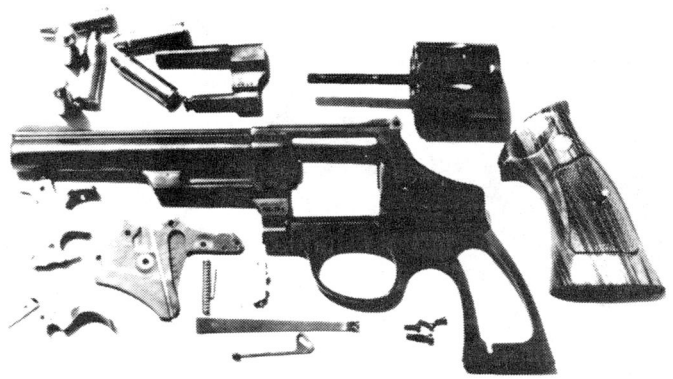

To find out, you take it apart and see how all the pieces work together. Analyzing the 4th Amendment involves the same kind of process.

undergoing continual change—you have to understand how the components of the 4th Amendment fit together and interact. You have to understand how the mechanism itself works before you can understand its capabilities and limitations. So let's disassemble the 4th Amendment and see what makes it tick.

> *The right of the people to be secure in their persons, houses, papers, and effects, against unreasonable searches and seizures, shall not be violated, and no warrant shall issue, but upon probable cause, supported by Oath or affirmation, and particularly describing the place to be searched, and the persons or things to be seized.*

There are 54 words to the 4th Amendment. Not all of them are mysterious components. Some are like the grips of a pistol: their purpose and use are obvious. Others require a closer look. So we're going to disassemble the 4th Amendment into 12 components and give them a closer look. Since it isn't possible (or wise) to try to consider these components out of context with each other, you should read the *entire* Amendment each time, but pay particular attention to those words which I've underlined, so you can begin to see how all the components fit together and interact.

SUBJECT OF THE AMENDMENT

> *The **right** of the people to be secure in their persons, houses, papers, and effects, against unreasonable searches and seizures, shall not be violated, and no warrant shall issue, but upon probable*

cause, supported by Oath or affirmation, and particularly describing the place to be searched, and the persons or things to be seized.

The Constitution has only 2 kinds of provisions: those which declare *duties,* and those which declare *rights.* Statutes which are subject to the Constitution cover such other interests as *privileges* (such as driving on public roads), *permissive activities* (use of parks and public beaches, for example), and *restricted activities* (zoning laws to control land use, for example). Anything conferred by statute can be *taken away* by statute. Anything conferred by the Constitution can only be taken away by Constitutional amendment.

Since the subject of the 4th Amendment is a *right,* it cannot be diminished or taken away by any statute—federal, state or local. The result is that the 4th Amendment has supremacy over any conflicting statute; if a legislative body attempts to give officers greater search-and-seizure authority than they possess under the 4th Amendment, the legislative act is subject to being declared unconstitutional.

On the other hand, a local government *may* enact statutes or local constitutional provisions which are *more restrictive* on law enforcement officials than the 4th Amendment. An example might be a law which forbids an officer to search a member of the opposite sex in in the security of a jailhouse.

The effect of this first component of the 4th Amendment, then, is to confer a Constitutional *right* which can be *enlarged* by local law, but not *diminished.*

WHOSE RIGHT?

The right of the **people** *to be secure in their persons, houses, papers, and effects, shall not be violated, and no warrant shall issue, but upon probable cause, supported by Oath or affirmation, and particularly describing the place to be searched, and the persons or things to be seized.*

Who has the 4th Amendment right? Everyone subject to US jurisdiction. Notice that the Constitution does *not* use the word "citizens," but uses the much broader word "people." This means that aliens, including illegal aliens, have the 4th Amendment right if they are subject to US jurisdiction (within the USA, on board US vessels, etc.). The right does not attach, however, until *after* a person passes through the point of entry. Border and customs searches are less restricted than searches occurring within the US. (See Chapter 4.)

Notice also that the Constitution does not say *"adult* people." Juveniles have the same 4th Amendment right as adults (although, as we will discuss later, youthful age may be a circumstance which might make a search or seizure reasonable).

Since a corporation is the legal equivalent of a person, a corporation has the 4th Amendment right, too. That means if you want to search a corporate headquarters for records of illegal operations, for example, you're bound by the same rules as for other similar searches.

WHAT IS THE RIGHT?

The right of the people **to be secure** *in their persons, houses, papers and effects,* **against unreasonable searches and seizures,** *shall not be violated, and no warrant shall issue, but upon probable cause, supported by Oath or affirmation, and particularly describing the place to be searched, and the persons or things to be seized.*

The right the 4th Amendment confers is the right not to be subjected to unreasonable searches and seizures. This is a *limited* right—notice that people do not have a right to be secure against *all* searches and seizures—only those that are "unreasonable." This means that as long as your search or seizure meets the prevailing criteria of reasonableness, it is not prohibited by the 4th Amendment. (The next 2 chapters discuss the distinctions between "reasonable" and "unreasonable" searches and seizures.)

WHERE IS THE RIGHT?

The right of the people to be secure in their **persons, houses, papers,** *and* **effects,** *against unreasonable searches and seizures, shall not be violated, and no warrant shall issue, but upon probable cause, supported by Oath or affirmation, and particularly describing the place to be searched, and the persons or things to be seized.*

You may not conduct an unreasonable search or seizure of a *person*. Since an arrest is a "seizure" of the person, you may not use any evidence obtained from the person (statements, hair samples, line-up ID, etc.) if you illegally arrested him, because such evidence would be the "fruit of the poisonous tree."

You may not conduct an unreasonable search or seizure within a *house*. This restriction has been held by the courts to extend to any structure or area which is part of the "curtilage" (that's a medieval word that means "courtyard"). The curtilage normally includes garages, sheds, barns, yards, and fenced gardens. And "house" includes a hotel or motel room, an apartment, a cabin, a tent, or any other place where a person lives—even if on a temporary basis.

The restriction as to searches and seizures of *papers* is fairly straightforward. But the term "effects" can cover a lot of territory: cars, boats, planes, luggage, containers, and dozens of other places where evidence might be concealed. Rather than try to enumerate all of the places where the 4th Amendment applies, the courts have decided to extend the scope to every place where a person might have a *reasonable expectation of privacy.*

If a person might reasonably expect privacy when he uses a public telephone booth, then the 4th Amendment applies there. If a person might reasonably expect privacy when he uses a public restroom stall, then the 4th Amendment applies there. If a person might reasonably expect privacy in the contents of a glove compartment, or a handbag, or a briefcase, then the 4th

"CURTILAGE"

The protected area around a house includes garages, sheds, barns, fenced areas and enclosed patios. While there is no set limit as to how far the curtilage extends, buildings more than 50 yards from the main house are often considered to be outside the curtilage.

Amendment applies there. (Chapter 3 is devoted to places where there is *no* reasonable expectation of privacy.)

WHO CAN CLAIM THE RIGHT?

The right of the people to be secure in their *persons, houses, papers, and effects, against unreasonable searches and seizures, shall not be violated, and no warrant shall issue, but upon probable cause, supported by Oath or affirmation, and particularly describing the place to be searched, and the persons or things to be seized.*

The US Supreme Court has recently held that the 4th Amendment right is a *personal* one—that is, it can be claimed only by someone whose *own* person or property was searched or seized. For example, you stop a car which contains a driver and a passenger. You search the car, which is owned by the driver, and you find and seize evidence which incriminates the *passenger.* This passenger has no standing to complain that the *driver's* 4th Amendment rights were violated, because the driver's rights are personal to him and can only be claimed *by* him.

The best way to analyze "standing" issues, is not to look just at ownership or rightful possession, but to consider whether the arrestee has reasonable expectation of privacy in the place searched or the thing seized. A person who has no reasonable expectation of privacy has no standing to object to the search and seizure, because that person's expectation of privacy has not been violated by the search.

Caution: *Some jurisdictions allow "vicarious standing."*

Local Rule: _____

_____

_____

SEARCH, OR SEIZURE?

The right of the people to be secure in their persons, houses, papers, and effects, against unreasonable **searches and seizures,** *shall not be violated, and no warrant shall issue, but upon probable cause, supported by Oath or affirmation, and particularly describing the place to be searched, and the persons or things to be seized.*

Many lawyers, judges and law enforcement officials use the phrase "search and seizure" in a careless, imprecise manner, as if they were talking about a single term. Searches and seizures often go hand-in-hand, but *they are 2 completely different acts.*

A *search* is an exploration to find things. If nothing is found, there isn't going to be any *seizure.* So as you can see, it's possible to have a search *without* having a seizure.

A *seizure* is taking custody or control over something (weapons, evidence, etc.). Although seizures often occur as the result of searches, it's possible to have a seizure *without* a search (for example, you find a bank moneybag lying on the sidewalk in front of the bank right after a robbery, and you seize it for fingerprints). Depending on the circumstances, there may be times when you have legal grounds for a seizure, but not for a search, and vice versa.

So even though you'll frequently see the phrase "search and seizure" throughout this book, and even though you may see officials who are supposed to know more about the law than you do misuse that phrase when *only* a search, or *only* a seizure is involved, you should always be alert to the fact that a search is not a seizure. And anytime you're testing your own conduct, ask yourself whether you have just a search, just a seizure, or both, and in which order. This will make it much easier for you to apply the proper *search* rules to the search, and the proper *seizure* rules to the seizure.

THE COP AS LAWBREAKER

The right of the people to be secure in their persons, houses, papers, and effects, against unreasonable searches and seizures, **shall not be violated**, *and no warrant shall issue, but upon probable cause, supported by Oath or affirmation, and particularly describing the place to be searched, and the persons or things to be seized.*

These 4 words are the source of the 4th Amendment exclusionary rule. Notice that the Constitution doesn't say what will happen *if* the right of the people is violated—it simply declares that the right "shall not be violated." As you know from studying criminal law, there's no point in making an act illegal if the law doesn't provide a punishment or other remedy for violations. Since the Constitution left a blank where the punishment or remedy for 4th Amendment violations should have been, the courts have taken it upon themselves to fill in the blank by saying that the remedy shall be exclusion of any evidence obtained through the violation.

This 4-word phrase is also the source of the terms "illegally-obtained evidence" and "unlawful search and seizure." The courts have as much as said that when officers violate a suspect's 4th Amendment right, the officers have violated the law, and their conduct should be described as "illegal" or "unlawful." (However, this is not the provision of law under which an officer can be criminally prosecuted. A prosecution for depriving a person of his civil rights arises under the US Code.)

SEARCH WARRANT BASIS

The right of the people to be secure in their persons, houses, papers and effects, against unreasonable searches and seizures, shall not be violated, and **no warrant shall issue, but upon probable cause,** *supported by Oath or affirmation, and particularly describing the place to be searched, and the persons or things to be seized.*

Here begins the second clause (or the second half) of the 4th Amendment. The first clause, which we've pretty well disassembled, is often referred to as the "unreasonable search and seizure clause." This second one is sometimes called the "search warrant clause."

Search warrants aren't handed out by judges (or magistrates) just for the asking. You can't just walk into the courthouse, say: "Judge, give me a search warrant for 218 Elm Street," and walk out with it. Before a judge can issue a valid search warrant, you have to tell him what you expect to find, and where, and why, and he has to agree with you that on the basis of what you know, you probably *will* find it there. (Probable cause requirements are covered in detail in Part Three.)

DID YOU SWEAR?

The right of the people to be secure in their persons, houses, papers, and effects, against unreasonable searches and seizures, shall not be violated, and no warrant shall issue, but upon probable cause, **supported by Oath or affirmation,** *and particularly describing the place to be searched, and the persons or things to be seized.*

When you apply for a search warrant, it isn't enough for you to simply "fill the judge in" on what you know. The requirement of an oath or affirmation is clearly spelled out, so reviewing courts insist on strict compliance with it. Therefore, if you supply the judge with your probable cause facts *in writing*, the writing must be in the form of a sworn affidavit. If you give your recitation of probable cause *orally*, you must be sworn, by a person who is authorized to administer oaths, before you begin to recount the facts which provide probable cause for issuance of the warrant (more specifics in Part Three).

COULD ANYBODY FIND IT?

> *The right of the people to be secure in their persons, houses, papers, and effects, against unreasonable searches and seizures, shall not be violated, and no warrant shall issue, but upon probable cause, supported by Oath or affirmation, and* **particularly describing the place to be searched,** *and the persons or things to be seized.*

When you go to get a search warrant for a case you're working, you're usually familiar with the place you intend to search: you've usually had the place under surveillance, or have been inside undercover, or have at least driven by once or twice. You know where you're going.

But the requirement of "particularity" in your description of the place means that any other officer—who is *not* already familiar with the place—must be able to read the search warrant and go directly to the right place, and be able to tell when he's found it. This means that a street address ("218 Elm") by itself is not enough. You have to describe the location and the appearance of the target in such detail that the right place will be searched, *even if the street address is incorrect, or there is no street address* (examples in Part Three).

TO SEARCH, OR ARREST?

The right of the people to be secure in their persons, houses, papers, and effects, against unreasonable searches and seizures, shall not be violated, and no warrant shall issue, but upon probable cause, supported by Oath or affirmation, and **particularly describing** *the place to be searched, and* **the persons** *or things* **to be seized**.

This language applies to *arrest* warrants, on its face. When you seize a person, you are arresting him. And note that this language says nothing about *searching* persons—it talks only about *seizing* them. Does this mean that you can't get a search warrant for a *person*?

No. If you intend to go to a suspect's house to search for evidence, and you also have probable cause to believe he might keep some evidence on his person, you may include him as a target of the search warrant. (Limited searches of some persons are implicitly authorized during the execution of the search warrant—see Part Three.)

The same requirements of particularity apply to the description of a person. You cannot simply call him by name—you must give a sufficiently-detailed description so that any officer serving the warrant can reasonably identify the right person. (See examples in Part Three.)

SEIZABLE THINGS

The right of the people to be secure in their persons, houses, papers, and effects, against unreasonable searches and seizures, shall not be violated, and no warrant shall issue, but upon probable cause, supported by Oath or affirmation, and **particularly describing** *the place to be searched, and* **the** *persons or* **things to be seized.**

If a search warrant is overbroad (sometimes called a "general search warrant"), it will not be upheld. You can't make the warrant so vague that it allows you to look for everything illegal—you must already know what you're looking for and where you will probably find it before you go in to serve the warrant. This means, once again, that you give the most definite, detailed description possible, and leave nothing in the warrant to the discretion or the interpretation of the serving officer. (See examples in Part Three.)

You have now read the 4th Amendment 13 times. I know criminal lawyers who can't make that claim (and I suspect the same is true of many judges). More importantly, you've seen the 4th Amendment disassembled into 12 component parts, and you've learned how these components fit together. This means that now you should understand how 4th Amendment law works when we get into practical applications of the various rules and their exceptions. And it also means that you'll be many steps ahead of the officer who simply tries to memorize the rules without a foundational understanding of the *sources* and *reasons* of the rules. You have a big advantage: you know what makes the 4th Amendment tick. □

NOTES ON LOCAL RULES

PART TWO

SEARCH AND SEIZURE WITHOUT A WARRANT

3

NO REASONABLE EXPECTATION OF PRIVACY

In *Katz vs United States,* the US Supreme Court said:

> *Searches conducted outside the judicial process, without prior approval by a judge or magistrate, are* <u>per se</u> *unreasonable under the 4th Amendment, subject only to a few specifically-established and well-delineated exceptions.*

In other words, if you conduct a search without a search warrant, it will be presumed to be unreasonable, and you can rebut this presumption only if you can show facts which put your search within one of the recognized exceptions. Obviously, this makes it extremely important for you to know what the recognized exceptions are.

The rule of thumb for all searches and seizures is simple: **"GET A SEARCH WARRANT IF AT ALL POSSIBLE."** If you *don't* get a search warrant, you're going to have to ask yourself *which* exception to the search warrant requirement you're going to rely on—and you're going to have to have a good answer, because that's precisely the question you're going to be asked by the prosecutor, the defense attorney, and the judge, anytime you make a warrantless search.

Since the vast majority of all searches and seizures are conducted without warrants, and since warrantless searches and seizures are presumed to be unreasonable, it's obvious that these large numbers of searches and seizures must fall into one of these categories: either they are held to be unreasonable (in which case the exclusionary rule gobbles up the evidence), or they are found to qualify for one or more of the established exceptions (in which case the evidence is saved).

Now, I don't have any statistics to show what percentage of warrantless searches and seizures are held to be unreasonable, but if my experience as a prosecutor is typical, it's a very substantial proportion. And I'm not just talking about "close" cases that could have gone either way, depending on the judge. I'm talking about large numbers of flagrant violations of the search warrant requirement by officers who didn't even offer a plausible attempt to invoke one of the established exceptions. I suspect that the chief reason for this situation is simply that many officers don't know what the exceptions are. Let's see if we can make sure that *you* never fit into that category.

As you saw during our disassembly of the 4th Amendment, there are some definite limitations on what the Amendment applies to. One of those limitations, as defined by the courts, restricts application of the 4th Amendment (and, thus, the search warrant requirement) to areas in which there is a *reasonable expectation of privacy*. This limitation creates a substantial field of exceptions to the 4th Amendment: if you search and seize an item or an area where there is *no* reasonable expectation of privacy, there is *no* 4th Amendment problem. Let's consider the most commonly-recognized examples.

PLAIN VIEW

If you see seizable evidence (such as contraband, fruits of a crime, or instrumentalities of a crime) in plain view, from a place where you have a right to be, you may seize the evidence without a search warrant in most cases. If a person has exposed an item to open view, he obviously did not retain a reasonable expectation of privacy.

EXAMPLES

SITUATION: *During a lawful carstop, you look through the front windshield and see the VIN. You jot it down and run it through NCIC while your partner is writing a citation to the driver for a traffic offense. You get a hit, and you arrest the driver when he is unable to produce registration or explain his possession of the car.*

RESULT: *Your observation through the windshield was a search, but you were able to see the VIN in plain view from a place outside the car where you had a right to be. This evidence is admissible.*

* * *

SITUATION: *You see a couple on a park bench rolling handmade cigarettes from a green leafy substance they take from a clear plastic baggie. You work your way around behind the park bench, and you smell the distinctive odor of burning marijuana. You approach the couple, seizing their cigarettes and the baggie which is lying on the bench beside them.*

RESULT: *All of your observations were made from a place where you had a right to be, and the suspects had exposed their cigarettes, their baggie and the fumes to public view and smell. They showed no reasonable expectation of privacy. Your observations and the items you seized are admissible. (Note: Before you can recognize the odor of burning marijuana, you must have previously smelled it, under circumstances where you knew what you were smelling. If necessary, you should arrange with the crime lab to observe a controlled burning of known marijuana to give you this background.)*

* * *

NO REASONABLE EXPECTATION/45

SITUATION: *You are dispatched to a home to settle a family disturbance. After an adult member of the household invites you into the living room, and as you are discussing the disturbance with the occupants, you see a sawed-off shotgun leaning against the wall in the corner of the room. You seize this illegal weapon.*

RESULT: *Since you saw seizable evidence in plain view from a place where you had a right to be, it is admissible.*

* * *

SITUATION: *You stop a pick-up truck for a broken taillight. As you walk up to it, you notice that something in the bed is covered with a tarp. You pull the tarp back and find a pile of car batteries, CB radios, and auto stereo decks, all with cut wires still attached. After further investigation, you establish that these items are stolen, you seize them, and you arrest the driver.*

RESULT: *Although you were in a place where you had a right to be, the items were not exposed to plain view until you uncovered them. You cannot rely on the plain view exception to justify your search and seizure, and under these facts, the stolen items are inadmissible.*

* * *

SITUATION: *A citizen calls you and tells you that his next-door neighbor is growing marijuana plants on the back patio, and that you can see them if you climb over the backyard fence and walk around to the end of the patio. You do so, and you find and seize marijuana plants growing in pots on the patio.*

RESULT: *Although the plants were in plain view from within the fenced backyard, you did not see them from a place where you had a right to be. Your observations and the plants are inadmissible. (This is precisely the kind of case in which you must obtain a search warrant.)*

ABANDONED PROPERTY

Once a person has abandoned his possessory interest in an item, he can no longer claim a reasonable expectation of privacy as to that item. However, if unlawful police activity *causes* a person to abandon the property, "fruit of the poisonous tree" problems will develop.

EXAMPLES

SITUATION: *You are walking on foot patrol in a commercial district. As you round a corner, you see two men exchanging items. When they look toward you, one of them shouts: "It's a cop! Run!" Both men take off running, and one throws a paper bag down on the sidewalk as he* flees. You retrieve the bag, chase the man down, and then look inside the bag, finding a stolen revolver and a packet of heroin, which you seize as evidence.

RESULT: When the suspect threw the bag down and ran away, he abandoned it, and he abandoned any expectation of privacy he might have had. His action in abandoning the property was motivated by his own consciousness of guilt, and not by any unlawful conduct on your part. The evidence is admissible.

* * *

SITUATION: You have a dealer's house under surveillance. You see him come out of the house with a full green plastic trash bag and deposit the bag on the curb, alongside other trash receptacles, for collection. Before the garbage truck arrives, you go through the trash and find used syringes, needles, and other paraphernalia with traces of methamphetamine. You seize these items.

RESULT: When a person puts something into the trash and puts it out for collection, he has abandoned any reasonable expectation of privacy in it. Search of the trash and seizure of evidence from it are not subject to the 4th Amendment. The evidence is admissible.

Caution: *If the trash receptacle is sitting in the suspect's garage or yard and hasn't yet been put out for collection, the suspect may be able to argue that he had not yet abandoned his expectation of privacy. A search warrant or other warrant exception may be necessary in such a case.*

LOCAL RULE: _____
_____
_____

* * *

SITUATION: *You see a known "mule" driving down the street, and you want to stop him and shake him. Even though you see no equipment violations or driving infractions, you red light him and honk your horn. He looks back over his shoulder, and you see a small package fly out the window of his car. After he stops, you retrieve the package, and you see that it has broken open and is spilling its contents, which you recognize as heroin. You seize this evidence.*

RESULT: *Even though the suspect abandoned this property by tossing it out onto the street, he did so in response to your effort to stop his car, and you had no legal grounds for doing so (under these facts). Since it was your unlawful act which caused him to abandon the heroin, you cannot rely on the abandoned property doctrine to save the evidence. It is inadmissible.*

NO STANDING

Another of the things we saw in the disassembly of the 4th Amendment was that a suspect has no standing to assert violations of another's rights, or to complain about the search or seizure of property not under his lawful control or possession. If a person does not own (or have legitimate custody of) an item, he cannot claim a reasonable expectation of privacy in it.

EXAMPLES

SITUATION: *As you are driving down the highway, you see a car and trailer fitting the description of a car and trailer stolen from a motel parking lot. By radio, you confirm that these are in fact the stolen vehicles. When your back-up unit gets in place, you turn on your red and blue lights and nudge the siren. The stolen car-trailer combination pulls off the highway immediately, comes to a quick stop, and the driver jumps out and runs into an orchard. He is soon caught and returned to the location of the stolen vehicles. You search inside the car and find a stolen pistol. You pull back the tarp covering the trailer bed and find stolen cameras and small appliances. You seize all of these items and charge the driver with vehicle theft and possession of stolen property (the vehicle owner is eliminated as a suspect).*

RESULT: *The suspect has no standing to assert a reasonable expectation of privacy as to a car and trailer which he had stolen. The evidence is admissible, without regard to whether or not you had probable cause to search the car and trailer.*

* * *

SITUATION: *You have a known burglar under surveillance. He drives across town to an apartment building and backs his car up to the entry. You follow him inside and see him trying the doors to eight apartments, all of which are apparently locked. Then you see him take a small shiny object from his rear pocket and stick it into the lock of an apartment door, jiggle it, and then open the door and step quickly inside. When you get to the apartment, you find the door slightly ajar. Looking inside, you see the suspect going through dresser drawers and tossing items of jewelry into a pile on the bed. You quietly walk in and capture the burglar without announcing your presence or purpose, even though your jurisdiction has a "knock-notice" statute.*

RESULT: *Since the burglar has no right to be inside the victim's apartment, he has no standing to complain about your method of entry. A burglar has no reasonable expectation of privacy in his victim's home. Your observations and seized evidence are admissible, without regard to whether or not you violated a knock-notice statute.*

OPEN FIELDS

The 4th Amendment does not protect obvious and notorious criminal activity conducted in an open place. If a criminal sets up an illicit operation in an unfenced, unposted, open area, which is not part of the curtilage of a house, he has not exhibited a reasonable expectation of privacy.

EXAMPLES

SITUATION: *You get an anonymous tip that an illegal whiskey still is being operated in an open wooded area outside of town. You drive into the area on public roads, walk through the woods, and find the still. You keep it under surveillance until you see the suspect arrive and make use of the still. You arrest him and seize evidence.*

RESULT: *This situation fits the open fields doctrine. The evidence is admissible.*

* * *

SITUATION: *The fish and game warden reports a suspected marijuana garden in a remote area, clearly visible from state lands. You accompany him to the area and see the marijuana patch, which is surrounded by a chicken wire fence that conceals nothing. When you see a suspect arrive and water the plants, you arrest him and seize the marijuana.*

OPEN FIELD

A makeshift marijuana "greenhouse" in the woods comes under the OPEN FIELDS doctrine. There is no reasonable expectation of privacy in such places.

RESULT: *The evidence is admissible under the open fields doctrine.*

* * *

SITUATION: *You get a tip from a confidential informant that stolen cars are being dismantled in a private salvage yard behind a rural gas station. You go to the area and find that the field behind the station is fenced with barbed wire, and is posted with "No Trespassing" signs. Climbing through the barbed wire, you make your way to an area set off by high shrubs and a high board fence. You climb the fence and see evidence of the dismantling operation. You call in VIN's and engine numbers on your pack set and confirm that they are stolen. You seize this property.*

RESULT: *The fencing, shrubs and posting in this case showed that the owner was exhibiting a reasonable expectation of privacy. This is not a case for the open fields doctrine, but is an example of a situation requiring a search warrant. The evidence is inadmissible.*

PUBLIC PLACES

If a person openly exposes criminal conduct or evidence to public view, he cannot claim a 4th Amendment expectation of privacy. This does not mean that all public places are automatically exempt from the search warrant requirement, however. A person is entitled to make use of public facilities and accommodations with the expected degree of privacy that normally would exist in such places.

EXAMPLES

SITUATION: *You know that a public restroom in a shopping mall is frequently used by homosexuals for unlawful public sexual activities. You arrange with mall authorities to hide in the ventilation duct above the toilet stall, from which you see two men engage in illicit lewd acts in the stall. You arrest them, on the basis of your observations.*

RESULT: *Since people normally expect privacy in a toilet stall and do not expect to be watched by a concealed observer, this warrantless search is not justified under the public places doctrine. Your observations are inadmissible.*

* * *

SITUATION: *You know that the public restroom in a city park is used by homosexuals for unlawful public activities. Park officials have removed the doors of the toilet stalls. Wearing plainclothes, you walk into the toilet and see one man seated on the stool and another kneeling between his knees, performing an act of oral copulation. You identify yourself and arrest the suspects.*

The degree to which a person has a protected expectation of privacy while using public facilities depends on the degree to which he shields his conduct or conversations from public exposure.

RESULT: *Since this criminal behavior was openly exposed to public view, there was no reasonable expectation of privacy. Your observations are admissible.*

* * *

SITUATION: *You learn that a neighborhood bookie uses a certain phone booth to transact his business. You put a bug in the booth, record his calls, and arrest him on the basis of the recordings.*

RESULT: *A person enjoys a reasonable expectation of privacy in a closed telephone booth. The recordings are inadmissible.*

* * *

SITUATION: *You learn that a bookie often uses one of the phones in an open bank of wall phones in the basement of the bus depot. You pretend to be using the next phone, and you overhear the bookie's end of several phone calls, indicating that he is accepting bets over the phone.*

RESULT: *Since the bookie carelessly exposed his conversation to be overheard in a public place, he did not exhibit a reasonable expectation of privacy. Your testimony as to what you overheard is admissible.*

NO REASONABLE EXPECTATION/57

IN JAIL

Prisoners are aware that they are being watched and listened to, and that their effects and living areas are subject to unannounced searches. Because of this knowledge, it is not reasonable for them to expect privacy in jail.

EXAMPLES

SITUATION: *You arrest a murder suspect and book him at county jail, where it is the policy to inspect all outgoing mail for escape plans, etc. Prisoners are informed of this policy. Your suspect writes a letter to his wife, in which he makes incriminating statements. You seize this letter as evidence.*

RESULT: *The suspect knew the risk of inspection of his letter. He had no reasonable expectation of privacy. The letter is admissible against him.*

* * *

SITUATION: *A jailed robbery suspect uses the jail telephone to call his brother. The jailer has an intercom station in the telephone room (not electrically connected to any telephone) which permits him to overhear what the prisoner is saying in the room. Prisoners are informed of this practice. The jailer hears the suspect tell his brother where to find a gun and mask and how to dispose of them.*

RESULT: *The prisoner could not reasonably expect to use the phone in complete privacy (or else he could plan escapes, etc.). The jailer's testimony as to what he overheard the suspect say into the phone is admissible.*

Caution: *Listening to a person's conversation with his* **attorney** *would violate the 6th Amendment right to counsel. Such overheard conversation would be inadmissible, and could raise other problems.*

* * *

SITUATION: *The jail electronically monitors each cell and records any conversation between prisoners. Prisoners in adjoining cells are overheard in this manner discussing the details of their respective crimes.*

RESULT: *The recording is admissible (assuming proper foundation and authentication), since prisoners do not have a reasonable expectation of privacy in jail.*

Caution: *A police "plant" may violate 5th and 6th Amendment rights. Statutes may establish "prisoner's rights" to privacy, restricting jail monitoring.*

* * *

NO REASONABLE EXPECTATION/59

SITUATION: *Assigned to jail duty, you get a tip from one of the prisoners that another prisoner has cocaine hidden in the bottom of his stick deodorant container. You search the prisoner's effects while he is at dinner, and you find the cocaine.*

RESULT: *The prisoner knows that his effects are subject to unannounced security searches. He has no reasonable expectation of privacy. The cocaine is admissible.*

EAVESDROPPING

The general rule is that if you eavesdrop briefly from a place where anyone could overhear a carelessly exposed conversation, you have not violated any reasonable expectation of privacy. Some courts have held, however, that prolonged eavesdropping is not acceptable.

EXAMPLES

SITUATION: *A motel clerk calls and tells you he overheard people in one of his rooms discussing a narcotics transaction. You go to the motel, and the clerk lets you into the unoccupied room adjoining the suspect's room. You listen beneath a connecting door and hear incriminating conversation.*

RESULT: *By discussing their illegal activities in such place and with such volume as to be overheard by neighbors, the suspects risked that their conversations would be reported to and overheard by police. There was no reasonable expectation of privacy. Your testimony as to what you heard is admissible.*

* * *

SITUATION: *You suspect that a known prostitute is using her hotel room for tricks. You rent the next room under an assumed name and set up shifts among 3 officers to listen through ventilation ducts and the poorly-insulated walls. After several days and nights, you have overheard four oral transactions for prostitution.*

RESULT: *Because of the prolonged and systematic nature of your eavesdropping, most courts probably would find that you had violated the suspect's reasonable expectation of privacy, and would not admit your testimony.*

LOCAL RULE: _____
_____
_____
_____
_____
_____

PHONE MONITORS

It is a serious federal violation for you to tap telephones without a court order. *Always* consult your legal advisor or prosecuting attorney if you need a tap. In most states, you may, however, listen to and record telephone calls if you have the *permission of one party* to the call. The theory for permitting this practice is that either party to a phone call risks the possibility that he might be misplacing his trust in discussing criminal activity with the other party. This negates any reasonable expectation of privacy.

EXAMPLES

SITUATION: *A housewife reports that she has been receiving obscene phone calls from an anonymous caller. With her permission, you attach a monitor and recording device to her receiver. You listen to and record 5 obscene phone calls.*

RESULT: *The suspect assumed an obvious risk that the victim would bring you in on her calls. He enjoyed no reasonable expectation of privacy. The recordings are admissible.*

* * *

SITUATION: *A confidential informant tells you a burglar will be calling him at 9:00 p.m. to tell him what kind of stolen goods he has for sale. The* informant agrees to let you monitor and record this phone call. During the conversation, the burglar incriminates himself in several residential burglaries.

RESULT: The burglar misplaced his trust in the informant. He cannot claim a reasonable expectation of privacy. *(Note: Unlike the jail situation, the 5th Amendment/Miranda problem does not apply to this phone call, since the suspect is not in custody. However, your coaching of the CI to draw the suspect into incriminating conversations could create an* **entrapment** *issue. As a tactical matter, it is preferable for the* **suspect** *to originate the call, and to do most of the critical talking.)*

Caution: *Privacy statutes in some states place procedural limitations on phone monitors. Be sure to check yours.*

LOCAL RULE:_____
_____
_____

PEN REGISTERS

When a person dials a telephone, he knows that the switching of his call is handled and recorded by telephone company personnel and equipment. Therefore, he does not have a reasonable expectation of privacy as

NO REASONABLE EXPECTATION/63

to the number he is dialing. Accordingly, no search warrant is required to install a pen register at the phone company to trace dialed numbers.

EXAMPLE

SITUATION: *Drug enforcement agents get word about a large shipment of cocaine and are given the phone number from which the distributor will be calling his street peddlers for pick-up arrangements. You have the phone company install a pen register to identify the numbers which the suspect calls. You trace these numbers, tail the street peddlers from their homes, and bust the operation.*

RESULT: *Since the distributor had no reasonable expectation of privacy as to the numbers he dialed, evidence you obtained through use of the pen register is admissible.*

Caution: *This is the federal rule, followed by most states. Check for your jurisdiction.*

LOCAL RULE: _____
_____
_____
_____
_____
_____
_____

WIRES

If you wire an officer or an informant and a suspect misplaces his trust by discussing criminal activity with the wired person, he cannot claim a reasonable expectation of privacy. If the person were not wired, he could nevertheless repeat anything he heard; the wire merely serves to allow recording of overheard conversations, so as to insure greater accuracy as to who said what.

EXAMPLE

SITUATION: *While working undercover, you are approached by a heroin dealer and invited to make a buy the following evening, inside a local movie theater. You wear a wire into the theater, and your conversations with the suspect during the transaction are transmitted to a recorder.*

RESULT: *The recording is admissible, just as your testimony is. The suspect misplaced his trust in you, and risked that you would testify against him. (Note: Be alert to entrapment problems.)*

Caution: *Some courts are automatically suspicious of anything that has electricity flowing through it, and they may require a court order, even though the accepted federal view is that wires do not violate any 4th Amendment expectation of privacy. Before you use one, verify the rule in your jurisdiction.*

LOCAL RULE: _____

_____

_____

OPTICAL AIDS

Anything which you have a right to see with the naked eye, in daylight, you also have the right to see with the aid of binoculars, telescopes and flashlights, day or night. No reasonable expectation of privacy is violated merely because you watch from a distant place of concealment, or because you illuminate your nighttime field of vision.

EXAMPLES

SITUATION: *You learn that a barber is dealing quaaludes and bennies from his shop. You know that if he spots you in the area, he'll get cautious. So you park three blocks away and look into his shop through the front window by means of high-powered binoculars. You see him counting, packaging and handing to his customers two different types of pills.*

RESULT: *Your observations are admissible. You would have had a right to stand on the sidewalk in front of his shop and look through the window at what was open to plain view in a public place. You do not lose that right merely because you increased*

66/SEARCH & SEIZURE HANDBOOK

When you need to stay out of sight, binoculars and telescopes may be used to help you see things you could lawfully watch from a closer vantage point.

the distance between yourself and the objects of your observation so as to avoid detection.

* * *

SITUATION: *You stop a car at night for a moving violation. As you approach the seated driver from the rear, you shine your flashlight into the interior of the car through the rear window. You see 4 new tires, with the manufacturer's sticker still on them, crammed into the rear floorboard, and a metal cash tray on the back seat. You know that similar items were reported taken from a burglarized service station earlier in the evening. Based on what you've seen with the aid of your flashlight, you investigate further and eventually arrest the driver for the burglary.*

RESULT: *An officer who has legitimately stopped a car is entitled to see anything that is in plain view from the outside. If it had been daylight, you would have been able to see the suspicious items through the rear window. You do not lose this right when the sun goes down, but may use a flashlight to help you see. Your observations do not violate a 4th Amendment expectation of privacy.*

Caution: *Use of binoculars or telescopes may not be approved when you are using them to see into a high-rise apartment or office which you could* *not see into from the sidewalk or street, nor when you are using them to see into a house or other building if you could not lawfully get close enough to look through the window.*

LOCAL RULE: _____

_____

_____

BEEPERS

You can use a beeper to help you maintain surveillance of a car, boat or plane that you could otherwise lawfully keep under constant visual surveillance. If the beeper is only an aid to help you avoid losing the vehicle in traffic, etc., there is no Constitutional search or seizure involved in its use. *Prolonged* use, however, may violate a right to privacy and require a court order.

EXAMPLES

SITUATION: *You learn that a marijuana dealer will be picking up some packages of imported marijuana at the airport. You stake out the public airport parking lot and see him arrive, park, and go inside the terminal. You place a beeper in his rear bumper while he is inside, and you follow him to his distribution point, using the beeper to allow you to stay out of sight as you tail him.*

NO REASONABLE EXPECTATION/69

RESULT: *He has no grounds for any 4th Amendment objection to this use of a beeper. You conducted no search or seizure, but merely used the beeper as a visual surveillance aid.*

* * *

SITUATION: *A chemical dealer tells you that a customer will be coming in to pick up several drums of chemicals which happen to be the primary components of manufacturing PCP. You plant a beeper in one of the drums in April, and you check the location by means of the beeper signal periodically through July. You do not attempt to keep visual surveillance of the drums throughout this period.*

RESULT: *Although there is no 4th Amendment search-and-seizure issue involved here, a federal court has held this kind of prolonged electronic surveillance to be an unlawful invasion of privacy, requiring a previous court order.*

TACTIC: *If you anticipate or find that prolonged reliance on a beeper will be necessary, seek a court order for its use.*

RUSE AND TRICK

While you may not employ a ruse or trick to accomplish a search, a seizure, or an entry that you were not otherwise lawfully entitled to accomplish, you may employ a ruse or trick to accomplish your lawful objective more peaceably, or to provoke a suspect into acting from his own consciousness of guilt. If he exposes his criminal conduct or evidence to you under a mistaken belief, he has waived his expectation of privacy.

EXAMPLES

SITUATION: *You make a lawful carstop. The driver gets out and comes to meet you. He is nervous, and tells you his passenger has a loaded handgun concealed under the front seat, and has been talking about wanting to "do" someone. The driver, who is also the registered owner of the car, voluntarily consents to allow you to search for the gun, but expresses his fear that if the passenger becomes suspicious, "he may do something crazy." You pretend to arrest the driver, and you approach the passenger window and tell the passenger you've arrested the driver for drunk driving and the driver has asked that the passenger drive his car home. You ask the passenger if he is willing to do so, and if he will step out and take a brief sobriety exam to make sure he is capable of driving. The passenger agrees and steps out. Once he is out of reach of the concealed weapon, you search for and seize the gun, and then arrest the passenger.*

RESULT: *The driver's consent allowed you to conduct a search in the driver's car for the concealed weapon. Your use of a trick to get the dangerous passenger away from the weapon merely allowed you to accomplish more peaceably what you were already entitled to do. This creates no 4th Amendment problem.*

* * *

SITUATION: *An informant whose tips have not always been reliable calls and tells you a suspect has been selling from a large stash of stolen hypodermic needles and syringes in his apartment, and that these things are going to be moved to a new location "sometime soon." The informant's reliability is insufficient for a search warrant, and you may not have time to develop corroborative information. So you phone the suspect at his apartment, pretend to be a former customer, tell the suspect you got busted and the cops are putting together a raid force and will probably be over soon, and that you just called your brother and told him to get over there ahead of the cops and help haul the stuff away in his green and white van.*

At about the time you hang up, an undercover officer in a green and white van screeches to a stop outside the suspect's apartment, honks the horn several times, and opens the rear door. The suspect comes running out, carrying 2 large cardboard boxes. As the officer helps load the boxes into the van, he can see hypodermic needles and syringes inside. When the suspect says: "That's all of them—let's get out of here," the officer identifies himself, arrests the suspect, and seizes the boxes.

RESULT: *All your ruse did in this case was to prompt a guilty person into incriminating himself from his own desire to avoid arrest. Since the suspect placed incriminating evidence into police custody under his mistaken belief that the officer was a criminal confederate, no search-and-seizure violation occurred.*

LOCAL RULE:_____

_____

_____

A single different fact in any situation may completely change your right to conduct a warrantless search or seizure, or to employ an investigative aid or device to assist your senses. Neither this handbook nor a search-and-seizure *encyclopedia* could possibly anticipate or cover all of the conceivable factual situations you may encounter. To be safe, therefore, you should keep the rule of thumb uppermost in mind: **"GET A SEARCH WARRANT IF AT ALL POSSIBLE."**

When it is not possible for you to get a search warrant, and the situation demands search-and-seizure action, the first question for you to ask yourself is this:

"Does the suspect have a reasonable expectation of privacy?" If the answer is *"no,"* you should identify in your mind the recognized doctrine which permits you to conduct a warrantless search or seizure.

If the answer is *"yes,"* you should then proceed to question number two: *"Even though the suspect has a reasonable expectation of privacy, is there an established exception to the search warrant requirement in this case?"* These exceptions are covered in the next chapter. ☐

NOTES ON LOCAL RULES

NOTES ON LOCAL RULES

4

SEARCH WARRANT EXCEPTIONS

You and I have to play by the rules. Crooks don't. They don't have to worry about legal niceties like jurisdiction, Constitutional rights, or probable cause. They go where they want to, when they want to. They commit their crimes wherever and whenever the opportunity presents itself—and that may be in the middle of town in the middle of the day, or it may be in the middle of the countryside in the middle of the night.

When your duties bring you into contact with criminal activity or evidence, you can't always call "time out" while you drive over to the courthouse and track down a judge and put together a search warrant. The criminal and the threatening situation won't always do you the favor of holding in place, while you get the "prior approval of a detached, neutral magistrate" for what you need to do.

So, even though the general rule is that searches without warrants are presumed unreasonable, there are a few established exceptions available to you. The courts have approved these necessary exceptions somewhat grudgingly, and each exception is narrowly applied. Moreover, the burden is always on the prosecution to prove that the case at hand qualifies under an exception. Sometimes, that's not an easy thing to do, so if you don't absolutely have to depend on one of the exceptions because of the circumstances, don't. **"GET A SEARCH WARRANT IF AT ALL POSSIBLE."**

THREE LEVELS OF CONDUCT

In the important 1983 decision of the United States Supreme Court in the case of *Florida v. Royer,* three distinct kinds of police/citizen "interactions" were identified. The court held that each level of contact has a distinct level of justification. Understanding and using the rules of this decision can make the difference for you of winning or losing cases which turn on search and seizure issues.

1. **CONSENSUAL ENCOUNTERS.** When an officer walks up to a citizen and without interfering with the citizen's liberty, talks to the person and looks at anything exposed in plain view, no detention has occured. In such cases there is nothing to be justified. The Supreme Court labelled this sort of contact a "consensual encounter," and held that since the citizen is free to stay or to leave, and to talk to the officer or remain silent, this encounter can take place *without any objective justification whatsoever.*

This means that when you see, for example, a known drug dealer, pimp or burglar parked on the street with the car window rolled down, you can walk up to the car and talk to the person. You may also notice anything in plain view, even though you have no "articulable suspicion" that he's involved in criminal activity and no probable cause for any search or seizure.

2. **DETENTIONS.** A "detention" occurs whenever you temporarily infringe on a suspect's freedom of movement, but not to the extent of immobilizing him or placing him under arrest. You're required to justify a detention with *articulable suspicion ("AS"),* which means that you have to give reasons for your suspicion that the detainee had committed or was about to commit some violation of the law. Note that this level of justification is *less* than probable cause to arrest.

A car stop is the kind of detention that requires articulable suspicion, (AS), as is stopping a pedestrian who is walking down the street or calling someone over to your patrol car when they are standing nearby. When you interfere with someone's liberty to this extent, be ready to give good reasons for doing it (or be prepared to lose any evidence resulting from the detention).

Possible ingredients of your articulable suspicion (AS) may be location, time of day or night, lighting conditions, inappropriate dress, visible weapons, carried objects, evasive conduct, flight, discarding evidence, traffic violations, truancy and curfew violations. The burden is on you to justify detentions with facts about your training, your experience, your observations and your conclusions that led you to suspect (and would lead any reasonable officer to suspect) the detainee's possible involvement in some particular criminal activity.

3. ARRESTS. An arrest or its equivalent (handcuffing, locking the suspect in your car-cage) requires *probable cause* ("PC"). This level of justification is more than an articulable suspicion of criminal behavior — it's a sufficient amount of information to warrant any reasonable officer in believing that the suspect committed a particular public offense.

Notice that *Florida v. Royer* makes it possible for you to begin with a consensual encounter, and from your conversation and observations establish enough articulable suspicion (AS) for a detention and patdown search, which may then supply enough probable cause (PC) for an arrest (seizure of the body) and resulting evidence.

Remember that if you fail to show in your report and your testimony that your level of intrusion had the corresponding level of justification, the search or seizure that produces evidence will *not* be valid, and the evidence will be suppressed ("fruit of the poisonous tree").

NOTE: *Many officers carelessly report or testify about "probable cause" when discussing encounters or detentions. DON'T DO IT! If you take on a higher burden of justification for your actions than the law requires, you risk getting a bad ruling if you can't meet the higher burden. Watch your terminology—and your sequence of events!*

ONE STEP AT A TIME

In most search-and-seizure situations, you do not start right off with a full measure of probable cause (PC) to conduct a full-scale, unlimited search and seizure. In most instances, you begin with minimal AS, just enough to warrant a slight intrusion on the suspect's 4th Amendment rights. From the initial encounter, you may gain additional AS for a still greater intrusion, and from this justified search, you find something which adds still more AS for a still greater intrusion. Working in this manner, one step at a time, you may eventually develop sufficient PC to justify extensive search and seizure, whereas if you "jumped the gun" the minute you came in contact with the suspect, everything you did might lack enough PC to survive a suppression motion.

EXAMPLES

SITUATION: *You see a car run a red light. After you stop it and see the driver jump out and start back toward you, you say to yourself: "This guy looks like a real dirt-bag. I'll bet he's hauling something in that trunk." You call to him to bring his keys and open the trunk. When he does so, you see a dead body. You immediately arrest and search the driver, and you find a bloody folding knife in his right front pocket.*

RESULT: *You had no AS to search the trunk, and the search of the suspect was tainted. The body and the knife are suppressed. You just blew a murder case.*

* * *

SITUATION: *You see a car run a red light. You stop the car and the driver comes back to the front of your police unit. You tell him you're going to issue a citation for the red light. You notice that instead of beginning to protest the ticket and argue with you the way most people do, he breathes a sigh of relief, gives a nervous little smile, and says: "Is that all you stopped me for? Uh, red light . . . uh, yeah, red light . . . ok, great!" When you ask for his license and he hands it toward you, you see bloodstains on his fingers. You say: "Are you hurt?" He quickly doubles up his fists and drops* *his hands to his sides in such a way that you can't see his fingers anymore.*

Then you notice bloodstains on his shoes, and you see that he's edging his right hand toward his right front pocket, which has a noticeable bulge in it. You frisk him and find the bloody knife, and then you take a closer look at his car. You notice that the rear of the car is lower than the front, and you see bloodstains around the trunk lock. You open the trunk and find the stabbed body.

RESULT: *All of the evidence is admissible. Each succeeding action by the suspect, and each succeeding observation by you, contributed to greater AS. By the time you frisked the suspect, you had reasons to believe he might have a weapon in his pocket and might have been involved in greater criminal activity than just busting a red light. By the time you opened the trunk, you had suspicion to believe that a dead or injured person might be locked inside.*

TACTIC: *Build your PC one step at a time, one fact on top of another. Unless your safety is threatened or some other emergency exists,* **exercise patience** *in establishing PC. Lack of patience by an officer who just can't wait to satisfy his curiosity is the second most common cause of evidence being suppressed (ignorance of correct search-and-seizure procedure is the first).*

"WHAT HAVE WE HERE?"

A ski mask, ammo, pistols, and currency inside bags in the trunk of a car can add up to a robbery conviction, IF you carefully built your PC for the search.

SEARCH WARRANT EXCEPTIONS/83

SCOPE OF SEARCH

All of the following exceptions to the search warrant requirement are *limited in scope*—you may never continue to search after the exception ceases to exist, and you may never search an area beyond the limited area where the exception applies. *Do not view these exceptions as giving you carte blanche to conduct an all-out, full-scale search.*

However, be alert to the possibility that one exception which justifies your initial, limited search may produce evidence which invokes *another* exception, giving you further search rights. For example, a homeowner consents to your searching the first floor of a 2-story house for a murder weapon. The scope of the consent limits the scope of your right to search. While downstairs, however, you hear screams and an explosion, like a gunshot, coming from upstairs. These facts invoke a second exception—lifesaving emergency—which now extends the lawful scope of your search to the upstairs area.

This second exception also has a limited scope of search: once you have discovered the source of the noises and have neutralized any life-threatening emergency, you may not continue to search unless a new exception has been invoked by the newly-discovered circumstances.

If you begin a justified search on the basis of a recognized exception and later feel a need to go beyond the scope of the exception, you are required to *obtain a search warrant.* A warrantless search or seizure which is outside the limited scope of the exception will result in the suppression of anything it produces.

The authorized scope of search for each of the following exceptions is illustrated with one or more examples.

EMERGENCY

You may conduct a warrantless search or seizure when you have probable cause to believe that a life-threatening or substantial property-threatening situation exists, and that there is no time to obtain a search warrant. You may not continue to search once the emergency ceases to exist. You may seize evidence or contraband which you notice in plain view while you are engaged in bringing the emergency under control.

EXAMPLES

SITUATION: *While patrolling a rural highway, you see a car pulled off the road, and an immobile—apparently unconscious—driver slumped over the wheel. Not knowing whether the driver is merely resting, or is passed out drunk, or has suffered a heart attack or other severe medical problem, you approach the car to see whether medical aid is needed. Unable to rouse the driver by tapping on the window of the locked door, you become more concerned, and you force the door open. The driver's eyes are glazed, and he fails to respond when you nudge him and call to him.*

You return to your car and request a medical rescue unit, and then go back to the unconscious

SEARCH WARRANT EXCEPTIONS/85

Medical-aid situations permit you to make limited, warrantless searches for medical information, identification, or substances which might have caused the medical problem. Contraband inadvertently discovered in this process is admissible under the EMERGENCY DOCTRINE.

driver. You check him for a medic alert bracelet; finding none, you go through his pockets and his attache case, looking for a medical warning card, or a medicine container, or the name of a physician or relative who could be contacted for information on a possible medical problem. During this process, you discover cocaine and marijuana in the attache case.

RESULT: *Since the object of your search was lifesaving information, rather than incriminating evidence, the emergency exception applies. The evidence is admissible.*

* * *

SITUATION: *You are dispatched to the emergency room, where you learn that Mr. Sallie just brought in his son, dead on arrival, a victim of starvation and dehydration. You also learn that Sallie has an 11-year-old daughter, and he refuses to tell you where she is, or what her condition is. You check records and get Sallie's LKA. When you get there, no one answers the door. Neighbors tell you that Sallie lives there, but they haven't seen either child in several weeks.*

Fearing that the 11-year-old daughter may be inside and may possibly be near death from starvation and dehydration, you break into Sallie's house and search for the girl. Although the girl is not inside, you find illegal weapons in a closet while you are looking for her. You also see potted marijuana plants in the kitchen, in plain view. Inside a cannister in the cupboard, you find packets of cocaine. You seize all of this evidence.

RESULT: *Because the weapons and marijuana came into view while you were legitimately engaged in a lifesaving search, the emergency exception will allow these items to be admitted. However, you exceeded the scope of the emergency exception when you looked inside the cannister (you could not expect to find the missing girl, nor any clue to her whereabouts, inside a kitchen cannister). The cocaine is inadmissible, under these circumstances, as the product of a warrantless search outside the scope of any legitimate exception.*

* * *

SITUATION: *You are on patrol on Sunday evening when you see smoke coming from the second-floor windows of a closed commercial building. You radio for the fire department. Although you have no reason to believe that anyone would be inside the building at this time, you break in the front door in order to locate the source of the smoke, intending to use any available fire extinguishers to help save the property. Once inside, you go from room to room, assessing the extent of the fire and looking for fire extinguishers. While in this process, you come across a chemical* laboratory, stocked with containers of various chemicals which you recognize as the components of PCP. You also see plastic baggies of white powder stacked on the end of a counter, and what appears to be a customer list lying next to this stack.

You continue with your fire-related activities until the fire department arrives and brings the fire under control. You then return to the laboratory, where you seize the baggies of suspected PCP and the list. You photograph the remainder of the items and the set-up. Fire officials tell you the arson investigator will be coming to the scene Monday morning (the next day), and you arrange to meet him. By the following morning, you have confirmed that the white powder you seized is PCP, and the narcs have identified several of the names on the customer list as known dealers.

You meet the arson investigator at the building, and you both go inside. He finds and seizes evidence of arson. You seize the remaining items of evidence from the PCP lab.

RESULT: *The baggies and customer list came into your view while you were legitimately engaged in property-saving emergency activities. You had probable cause to suspect that these items were contraband and instrumentalities of crime. They are admissible under the emergency exception.*

Once the fire was extinguished, the emergency ceased to exist. Between Sunday evening and Monday morning, there was ample time for both you and the arson investigator to obtain search warrants. *Your warrantless searches and seizures on Monday morning are not covered by any exception. The evidence taken on this occasion by you and the arson investigator is inadmissible.*

* * *

SITUATION: *A citizen calls the station and says: "I've killed one of your cops. Come and get me." You are the first to arrive at the given address, and you see a police car parked in front of the house. A man in an undershirt and jeans is holding open the door, and motions you to come in. The shotgunned dead officer is lying on the floor, just inside. The man who met you at the door says: "I'm the one who called. I did it. I just don't care anymore." As you cuff him to a heavy table, back-up officers arrive. You immediately begin a room-to-room search for additional suspects. You find no one else, but you do find a shotgun lying on the floor beneath the bed. After properly measuring, marking and photographing, you seize the shotgun.*

Homicide investigators arrive within minutes and begin going through the house again. Their search turns up shotgun shells in a desk drawer and narcotics in a nightstand drawer.

RESULT: *You are not required to take the suspect's word that he was the killer, nor to jeopardize your own safety by assuming that no other armed and dangerous suspects are concealed within the house. Your initial room-to-room search was not unlawful, and since you found the possible murder weapon in a place where you could lawfully look for a hiding suspect, it is admissible.*

Although there once was a recognized "homicide scene" exception to the search warrant requirement, the Supreme Court has eliminated it. The search conducted by the homicide investigators in this situation took place after the emergency was neutralized, and it went into places where no armed suspect could possibly be hiding. The evidence seized by the investigators is inadmissible because it resulted from a warrantless search outside the scope of any recognized exception.

* * *

You are most likely to benefit from the emergency exception for warrantless searches and seizures in cases where you inadvertently discover evidence while dealing with an unconscious person, an incoherent person, a medical aid situation (diabetics, overdose cases, attempted suicides, traffic accident victims, and victims of violence), an immediate, life-threatening peril (shots or screams heard, fight noises, blood trails, explosions, and fires), or an immediate *and* substantial property-threatening peril (fire, explosions and natural disasters).

SEARCH WARRANT EXCEPTIONS/91

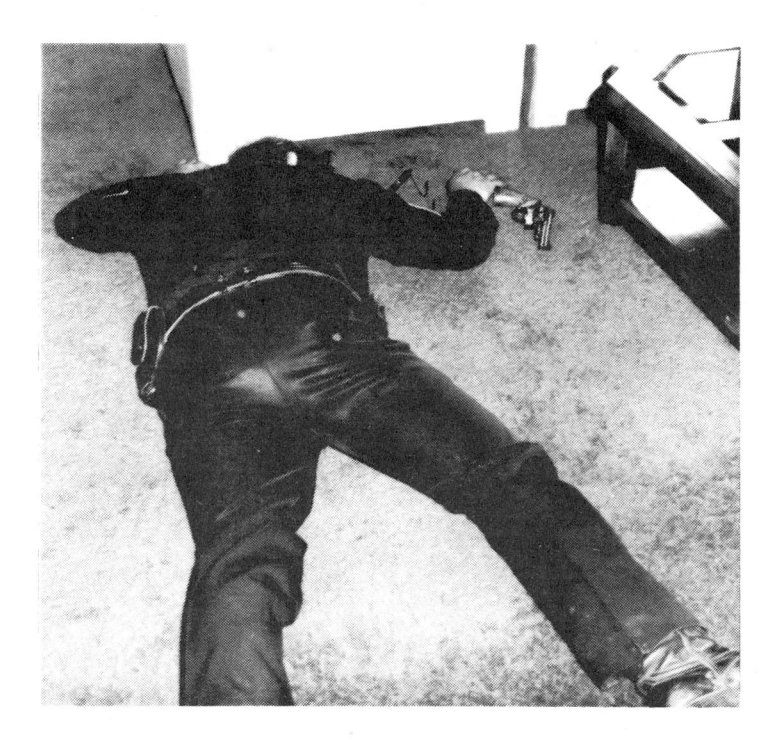

You could cause the loss of valuable evidence in an officer homicide case if the sight of a slain fellow officer throws your emotions out of control. There is no "homicide scene" exception to the search warrant requirement. If the emergency is over, you must contain the scene and obtain a search warrant.

Remember to confine your searching/seizing activities to places where your emergency activities are warranted and to cease searching once the emergency ends. If additional searches and seizures are indicated by what you've found, you must obtain a search warrant if no other exception applies to the extended search.

OFFICER PROTECTION

You may make a warrantless search for weapons and seize anything which reasonably appears to be a potential weapon, or any contraband which inadvertently comes into your view during your weapons search, whenever you have probable cause to believe that the person you are dealing with may be armed and dangerous. The scope of a protective search is limited to the *person* and places *within arm's reach* where the person might reach for a concealed weapon.

Factors which may contribute to PC for a protective search include darkness, remote location, outnumbered officer, relative physical sizes of the officer and the other person, reason for the contact, encountered hostility, excess clothing (heavy coat on a warm day), visible bulges in clothing, excess nervousness or excited state, visible recent injuries, torn or bloodstained clothing, quick sudden movements, apparent efforts to adjust clothing or conceal something, a known record of violence, and recent reports that the suspect is armed and dangerous.

SEARCH WARRANT EXCEPTIONS/93

EXAMPLES

SITUATION: *You are dispatched to an apartment on a family disturbance call. When you arrive, the wife invites you inside and says that her drunken husband has been breaking things and yelling and cursing, and has been in the bathroom for several minutes. As you are talking to her, the husband comes into the room, looks at you, and yells: "Fuckin' bitch has got the pigs on me!" As he turns and runs into the bedroom, the wife whispers: "He's got a gun in there!"*

You run after the husband and see him standing beside the bed, emptyhanded. You pat him down and feel a long, hard object in his front pants pocket. Believing that this may be either a knife or a gun, you reach into his pocket and remove the item, which turns out to be an illegal switchblade knife. Continuing your pat-down search, you feel a soft, bulging item in his shirt pocket. You retrieve this and find it to be a baggie of marijuana.

You search within arm's reach of the suspect and find more marijuana as you open the nightstand drawer, and a .22 automatic under the mattress on the bed. You notice that the serial number has been ground off the weapon, in violation of state law. You seize all of these items of evidence and arrest the suspect.

RESULT: *You were justified in conducting a pat-down search of the suspect in his bedroom to insure your* own safety. Your PC for this limited search includes the nature of the call (domestic violence), the suspect's expressed hostility on seeing you, his sudden action in turning and running into another room, and his wife's warning to you that he had a gun in the room. The long hard object you felt in his pants pocket was reasonably identifiable as a potential weapon, so you were justified in reaching in and removing it for examination. Once you saw that it was, in fact, an illegal knife, it was subject to seizure. The knife is admissible.

You did not immediately arrest the suspect on discovery of the knife, but continued your search for the gun. The soft bulge in his shirt pocket was not reasonably identifiable as any kind of potential weapon; therefore, you cannot justify removing and examining it on the basis of protective search. Under these facts, that marijuana is inadmissible.

Your searches of the nightstand drawer and the bedding, both areas within the suspect's reach where he might pull a concealed weapon, were justified as within the scope of your protective search. The gun is admissible, and since this quantity of marijuana inadvertently came into your view when you opened the drawer to look for a gun or other weapon, it is admissible.

* * *

SEARCH WARRANT EXCEPTIONS/95

SITUATION: *You make a lawful traffic stop at night in a deserted area. As you approach the car, you see the driver (who is the sole occupant) bend forward out of sight, and then sit up again. You have also noticed that while the car is muddy and dirty, the rear plate is clean. You order the driver out of the car, and he immediately yells: "Jesus Christ! What now? Can't you guys ever do anything but hassle people? No wonder so many cops get shot!"*

You pat the driver down for weapons and find nothing. You tell him you stopped him for a traffic violation and are going to issue a citation. You order him to stand in front of the headlights of his car, with both hands on the hood. While he is in this position, you run your hand along under the driver's seat and feel nothing. You fold the driver's seat forward and feel beneath the rear seat, where you find an illegal billy club, which you seize.

RESULT: *You had sufficient PC to warrant a pat-down for your own safety (dark, deserted area; suspicious movement by the driver, who could have been reaching under the seat for a gun; a possible stolen vehicle or stolen plates, which might mean the driver could have a motive to harm you to prevent arrest; and vocal hostility in the driver's attitude). If you had found weapons during this pat-down, they would have been admissible.*

Likewise, any weapons under the driver's seat would have been admissible, since your *protective search can extend to areas within arm's reach (even though the driver was at the front of his car at the time and could **not** have reached under the front seat, he could have done so once the citation was issued and you were walking back to your car).*

Since you went beyond the driver's reach when you searched beneath the rear seat, you exceeded the scope of the protective search exception. Under these facts, the billy club is inadmissible.

STOP AND FRISK

You may stop a person for investigation if you have articulable suspicion to believe he may be engaged in criminal activity. You may conduct a pat down of his outerclothing, in an attempt to discover weapons, for your own safety and the safety of the public, if you have articulable suspicion to believe he is potentially dangerous.

EXAMPLES

SITUATION: *You see a pedestrian in a shopping area, carrying a brown paper bag, which apparently has something inside it. He is stopping people on the sidewalk, showing them the contents of the bag, and saying something to them. The people are then shaking their heads and walking on. Suspecting that this man is trying to sell narcotics or stolen property, you stop him and take the bag* away from him. Looking inside, you find a revolver, which you later determine to be stolen.

RESULT: These facts have been held to be insufficient to give you PC for the investigative stop and search. Your observations could just as easily be explained by someone trying to give away a kitten or a puppy, or to sell his own property. Since you lacked PC to believe the suspect was engaged in criminal activity, the revolver is inadmissible.

* * *

SITUATION: On a warm summer night, you see a car with its headlights off slowly pull up beside a liquor store, a few minutes before closing time. The lone driver slouches down in the seat and sits there for several minutes. You can see exhaust smoke, indicating that the motor is running. As the storekeeper begins turning out lights around the store, the driver gets out of his car. He is wearing excessive clothing and looking back and forth.

Before the driver gets to the door of the liquor store, you intercept him. You explain why you've stopped him and he tells you he was just going in to buy a bottle. You pat down his outer clothing and feel a hard object beneath his jacket, at the waist. You ask him what that is and he says it's his wallet. You reach in and withdraw a loaded revolver.

RESULT: *The suspect's activities and explanations were sufficiently suspicious to warrant his detention and frisk. The revolver is admissible.*

* * *

SITUATION: *You are on duty at the turnstyle entrance to a city-owned hall used for a rock concert. You are looking for narcotics and minors in possession of alcohol. As teenagers enter, you inspect their packages, arresting anyone who has narcotics or unlawful alcohol.*

RESULT: *These are exploratory searches, not supported by PC to search. The narcotics and alcohol you seize are inadmissible.*

TACTIC: *Since the city owns the concert hall, the city should consider making "consent to search" a condition of the sale of concert tickets. Since many of these events characteristically produce drug violations and anonymous bomb or assassination threats, a uniform search for weapons and contraband may be upheld as a condition of the license (ticket) to enter the building.*

FLEETING TARGETS

You may conduct a warrantless search of a fleeting target (automobile, motor home, boat or airplane) if you have probable cause to believe that it contains seizable items. The rationale for this exception is that a mobile target may be gone by the time you get back with a search warrant—and a person has a reduced expectation of privacy in a vehicle as compared with his home or business. The scope of the search is defined by the size and nature of the contraband or evidence believed to be inside: you may search in any area, and inside any container, that might be capable of concealing the property you have PC to search for. In *US v. Johns,* the U.S. Supreme Court held that such a search was reasonable, even though the suspect's truck had been impounded by the DEA for three days.

EXAMPLES

SITUATION: *You are on 1-man patrol and make a lawful traffic stop on a car which contains 3 people. For your safety, you order all 3 people out of the car. As they climb out, you see a set of brass knuckles on the front floorboard. You later seize this illegal weapon and arrest the person who you determine to be the possessor.*

RESULT: *In 1977, the Supreme Court held that once you have lawfully stopped a car, you can order the occupants out for your own safety. This action does not require any specific indications of criminal activity, but may be done as a routine precaution against surprise assault. Since the brass knuckles came into your view during this authorized action, and since you could not reasonably expect to return to the vehicle later with a search* warrant and find the evidence still there, the brass knuckles are admissible.

* * *

SITUATION: *You stop a lone driver for DWI. As you are helping him out of the car, you see 4 loose rounds of .45 caliber ammo lying on the front seat. The presence of ammo suggests the presence of a gun, so you pat the driver down and find a loaded clip, but no gun. After you secure the driver, you search the interior of the car and find a .45 automatic concealed under the right front passenger seat. State law forbids carrying a concealed handgun within a vehicle, so you seize the gun and arrest the driver.*

RESULT: *The presence of ammo and a loaded clip are strong indications that there was a gun somewhere in the car. You had PC to search and to seize the gun when you found it.*

Note: *In this search, you were not limited to the "arm's reach" scope of the* **protective** *search. In this case, you had PC to believe that evidence of a crime was in the car, and you were searching a fleeting target for* **that** *specific evidence. Remember that the "arm's reach" restriction applies to* **precautionary** *searches; if you have PC to search a fleeting target for any seizable items, you may search the <u>entire</u> passenger compartment, without*

SEARCH WARRANT EXCEPTIONS/101

regard to the "arm's reach" rule. You may also search the glove compartment or trunk if you have specific PC to believe that evidence may be there.

* * *

SITUATION: *You are parked near an intersection in a marked police car. You see a car run the stop sign, and you pull in behind him. When you turn on your overhead lights and honk, the driver looks back toward you, then seems to be handling something on the seat beside him. He does not increase or decrease his speed for a full 2 blocks, before finally yielding when you turn on the siren. He quickly jumps out of the car with a partially-filled pillowcase, throws it into his trunk, then slams the trunk lid closed as you approach. You take his keys, open the trunk, retrieve the pillowcase, and search it, finding assorted narcotics.*

RESULT: *The suspect's actions gave you PC to believe that he was attempting to conceal contraband in the trunk. Since he would otherwise have been free to go after signing the citation for the stop sign, your search of the trunk comes under the "fleeting target" exception for warrantless searches. The narcotics are admissible.*

* * *

FLEETING TARGET?

If you have PC to believe a moving vehicle contains seizable property, you may conduct a warrantless search. However, if the vehicle is parked and unoccupied and circumstances permit, you must obtain a warrant, since a stationary vehicle is not "fleeting."

SEARCH WARRANT EXCEPTIONS/103

SITUATION: *At the scene of a lawful carstop, you arrest the driver and one of the 2 passengers on outstanding traffic warrants. The driver turns the car over to the remaining passenger. You ask the arrestees if they want to take anything from the car with them. They ask for jackets from the trunk. You open the trunk, search the jackets, and give them to your arrestees. You then notice a piece of hand luggage and a small metal box behind the spare tire. You pull these items out, open and search through them, and find stolen weapons and narcotics, which you seize.*

RESULT: *You had no PC to believe that any seizable items were in these containers. Therefore, you cannot invoke the "fleeting target" exception for these warrantless searches. Under these facts, the evidence is inadmissible.*

* * *

SITUATION: *A woman calls the station and says her ex-husband just left in a described pick-up truck, and that he has a "load" of marijuana in the bed, under a snap-on cover. You hear the broadcast and see the truck. You stop it, smell a recognizable odor of marijuana through the cover, unsnap the cover, and see 2 plastic tubs full of processed marijuana. You arrest the driver and secure him. You then look into the cab and see a closed attache case lying on the floorboard. Suspecting* *that this case may contain customer lists or transaction information, you open it and find such papers. You seize these items and impound the truck as a vehicle used to transport narcotics.*

RESULT: *You had sufficient PC for your warrantless search of the truck bed under the "fleeting target" exception. However, once the suspect was in custody and the attache case was under your exclusive control, you needed a search warrant before opening the case. The documents you found inside are not admissible under the "fleeting target" exception. Proper procedure under these facts would have been to seize the briefcase as a probable source of evidence and seek a warrant to look inside it.*

* * *

You may search any area of a fleeting target where you have probable cause to believe seizable items will be found. However, if you are taking an occupant into custody and wish to search small, movable containers, such as handbags, briefcases, trunks, luggage, toolboxes, cartons, medicine vials, snuff boxes, etc., the proper procedure is to take these containers into custody and obtain a search warrant before opening them and looking inside.

SEARCH WARRANT EXCEPTIONS/105

INCIDENT TO LAWFUL ARREST

You may make a warrantless search or seizure of the person and clothing of someone you have lawfully arrested for a bookable offense. You may also search the area within arm's reach for weapons, or to prevent the arrested person from disposing of evidence or obtaining means of escape.

EXAMPLES

SITUATION: *You stop a driver for speeding. You are not authorized to book for this violation, but must release the driver on his written promise to appear. You search him before releasing him, and you find a hypodermic kit in his coat pocket.*

RESULT: *This evidence is not admissible, because you were not authorized to take the driver into custody. In order to make a valid warrantless search incident to arrest, the arrest must be for a bookable offense.*

* * *

SITUATION: *During a lawful carstop, you arrest the driver on outstanding traffic and misdemeanor warrants. Before transporting him, you search his clothing. You find a packet of heroin inside his boot top.*

INCIDENT TO ARREST

You may make a limited, warrantless search if you have lawfully arrested the suspect for a bookable offense, and your search is not unnecessarily delayed.

SEARCH WARRANT EXCEPTIONS/107

RESULT: *The heroin is admissible. This is a legitimate warrantless search incident to arrest.*

* * *

SITUATION: *You are dispatched to a disturbance call and are admitted to an apartment by the female resident. She tells you her former boyfriend is in the bedroom and refuses to leave. She wants him out of her apartment because, she says, "He thinks this place is a shooting gallery. I don't want him to OD here. Get him out." You go into the bedroom and see symptoms of heroin use and influence on the boyfriend, who is sitting on the edge of the bed. You arrest him for trespassing and use of opiates. You search him and find a bindle of heroin. You search under the pillow, within his arm's reach, and find an outfit. You seize these items of evidence.*

RESULT: *This evidence is admissible as the product of a search incident to a lawful arrest. You were entitled to search any place of concealment where the arrestee could have reached to destroy evidence or obtain a weapon.*

* * *

SITUATION: *You lawfully arrest a woman, with an arrest warrant, as she steps off a plane from Mexico. You suspect that she is smuggling cocaine into* *the country. Your female partner searches the arrestee's clothing and finds nothing. You seize the "overnight case" which she carried off the plane, open and search it, and find 2 lbs. of cocaine.*

RESULT: *Any evidence which the clothing search might have turned up would have been admissible. However, once the arrestee was in custody and police officers had exclusive control of the "overnight case," a search warrant was required before opening it. The cocaine is inadmissible. This search was not of the* **person** *or* **clothing** *of the arrestee, and the case had been removed from arm's reach. The exception for warrantless search incident to arrest does not apply.*

* * *

SITUATION: *While on daytime patrol, you see a man carrying a portable TV set down the alley behind an apartment complex that experiences numerous burglaries. You arrest the man for suspicion of burglary, and your search of his clothing reveals burglary tools. You are unable to determine whether or not the TV was in fact taken in any burglary.*

RESULT: *The evidence you seized is inadmissible because you had not established sufficient PC to arrest the man before you did so. Since the* arrest was unlawful, you cannot rely on the exception of search incident to a **lawful** arrest to justify your warrantless search.

* * *

SITUATION: *You lawfully arrest a robbery suspect in a motel room after being invited in. You cuff him and place him in the back of your patrol car and take him to the station. After several hours of interrogation, you remember that you did not search the suspect or the motel area within arm's reach of the place where you arrested him. You search him and find a small amount of marijuana. Leaving the suspect in a holding cell, you return to his motel room and search the arm's reach area where you arrested him. You find more marijuana. When you return to the station, you learn that your arrestee has been eliminated as a robbery suspect. You book him for possession of marijuana.*

RESULT: *The marijuana (both quantities) will not be admissible as a product of a search incident to lawful arrest. The courts have held that "incident to" means* **closely related in time and location** *to the arrest. Your searches of the suspect and his motel room were not closely related in time or location to the arrest. The exception does not apply.*

SITUATION: *You lawfully arrest a suspected felon in his neighborhood, where a large, hostile crowd quickly forms. You cuff the suspect and haul him away from the area. As soon as you reach a place of safety, you take him out and search him, finding counterfeit money in his shirt pocket.*

RESULT: *Your search was delayed and removed from the location of the arrest only because of an urgent necessity. Since you conducted the search as soon as was reasonably practical following the arrest, it will still be considered as being "incident" to the arrest. The evidence is admissible.*

* * *

Whenever you seek to justify a warrantless search or seizure as being incident to a lawful arrest, be sure that the suspect has been placed under arrest *before* the search occurs, that he is arrested for a *bookable offense,* that the search was limited to the suspect's *person, clothing* and *arm's reach* area, that your arrest was *lawful,* and that the search was *closely related* in time and location to the arrest.

Unless some emergency or other exception applies, you should *not* rely on searching incident to a lawful arrest if a *bodily invasion* is required. Always seek a search warrant and the assistance of medical personnel for strip searches, vaginal and anal searches, prostate massage, fluid extractions (except blood alcohol tests), and stomach pumps.

SEARCH WARRANT EXCEPTIONS/111

HOT PURSUIT

If you are in lawful, fresh, and close pursuit of a fleeing suspect, you may make a warrantless entry into anyplace where he seeks refuge, and you may conduct a warrantless search and seizure of his person, clothing, and arm's reach area. This search authority is the same as for protective searches and search incident to lawful arrest (presumably, you will arrest the pursued suspect upon capture). The primary difference in the "hot pursuit" exception is that it allows you to make warrantless *entries* into places that would otherwise require a warrant, or another exception.

EXAMPLES

SITUATION: *As you are driving on patrol, an excited merchant flags you down, points to a speeding car, and says: "Those guys just robbed me! They've got shotguns!" You give chase with red lights and siren, and the car speeds up, making frequent turns, blowing red lights, and causing near-collisions. You lose sight of the car momentarily as it turns a corner, and as you round the corner, you see the car stopped in the yard of a house, both car doors standing open, and one man running into the house through the front door.*

Your backup officers are arriving as you leave your car and run toward the front door of the house. You find the door closed, but unlocked. You and several officers open the door and look inside. The front room is empty. You go inside and begin a careful room-to-room search. You find 3 suspects hiding in a bedroom closet. You arrest, cuff, and remove them. Not knowing whether other armed suspects are still concealed in other parts of the house, you complete a thorough search and find shotguns and a paper bag of money under the bed. You seize these items.

RESULT: The "hot pursuit" exception covers your warrantless entry into the house, and your seizure of the fruits and instrumentalities of the crime is covered by several exceptions (hot pursuit, incident to lawful arrest, protective search, and plain view). The evidence is admissible.

* * *

SITUATION: You've been looking for Danny, the dope dealer, for several weeks. While you are on foot patrol in a downtown area one day, a snitch comes up to you and tells you he just saw Danny run into a hotel across the street. You dash across the street, confirm Danny's room number from the desk clerk, run up the stairs to the room, and open the door. You see Danny counting money at the coffee table, with a small stack of heroin packets and balloons lying on the table. You arrest Danny and seize all this evidence.

RESULT: *This evidence is inadmissible. You made a warrantless entry which does not come under the "hot pursuit" exception (nor any other exception, on these facts); you were not actually in close pursuit of Danny, because you never saw him, he never saw you, and there was no actual* chase *or* pursuit *involved. The fact that Danny* ran *into his hotel, and the fact that you* ran *in order to find him, did not make this a close pursuit—the element that is missing is his* fleeing *from the authority of the law.*

* * *

What happens if you are in hot pursuit of a fleeing suspect, you lose him, and several hours later you find out where he's holed up? Can you then make a warrantless entry to get him, or do you need arrest and search warrants? The answer depends partly on the attitude of the courts in your jurisdiction, partly on the length of the time interval between your losing and relocating him, and partly on the nature of the crime he is suspected of committing.

EXAMPLES

SITUATION: *You are pursuing an indecent exposure suspect on foot. He jumps into a car and flees. You note the license number. When you get back to your patrol car, you run the number, but the computer is down, and you don't get a* make on the plate for 5 hours. When you get the suspect's address, you go directly to his home. No one answers your knock on the door, so you look through the window. You see the suspect sitting on the couch. He sees you and runs into another room. You go back to the front door, push it open, go inside, and arrest the suspect. While inside, you see the discarded clothing that he was wearing when he exposed himself. You seize this clothing.

RESULT: *In most jurisdictions, your entry would not qualify as a "hot pursuit" exception. The crime was not one which placed the public in continuing danger with the suspect at large, the time interval of 5 hours was so substantial that you could have sought a warrant while awaiting the address, and there was little chance of your preventing the destruction of vital evidence by your warrantless entry and seizure. The safest assessment of these facts is that they do not show a fresh, close pursuit. The evidence is not likely to be admissible.*

* * *

SITUATION: *You are in hot pursuit of a masked and armed perpetrator of a bank robbery in which a teller was shot and wounded. You lose the car in traffic. You run the plate and get an LKA within 1 hour. You go there and spot the car parked behind the house. No one responds to your* *announcements at the front door, although you hear noises within. You and other officers break open the door, find the suspect hiding behind the couch, and retrieve a mask, gun and bank money from areas within his arm's reach.*

RESULT: *In most jurisdictions, your entry would qualify as a "hot pursuit" exception. The crime was a serious one, the public might be in continuing danger while the armed and dangerous perpetrator remained at large, the time interval was relatively short (and probably inadequate to put warrants together), and your entry was reasonably necessary to prevent the disposal of evidence of the crime. This evidence is most likely to be admissible.*

* * *

In "hot pursuit" cases, you must remember to confine your searches to the scope of the exception. Once the suspect has been captured, and your protection has been assured, and the limited search has occurred, you must cease search-and-seizure activities unless other exceptions extend your search rights, or until you have obtained a warrant.

The more *serious* the crime and the *shorter* the time interval in an interrupted pursuit, the more likely an eventual warrantless entry and search will be *upheld.* The more *harmless* the offense and the *greater* the interruption of your pursuit, the more likely an eventual

116/SEARCH & SEIZURE HANDBOOK

warrantless entry and search will be declared *invalid.* Whenever circumstances and the public safety permit, **SEEK A WARRANT** once your pursuit has been substantially interrupted (more than a half-hour's interruption is probably substantial in most cases).

> **Note:** *If no warrantless entry is involved, an interruption does not change your rights under the "hot pursuit" exception. For example, you pursue a suspect, lose him, and see him in traffic (or a public place) many hours later. You simply* **resume** *your hot pursuit at this point.*
>
> **Caution:** *Many jurisdictions limit the "hot pursuit" exception to cases where you have PC to believe the fleeing person is* **armed** *and has committed a dangerous* **felony.**

LOCAL RULE: _____

_____

_____

IMMINENT DESTRUCTION OF EVIDENCE

You may make a warrantless entry and conduct a warrantless search or seizure if your doing so reasonably appears necessary to prevent the imminent destruction of evidence, *and* if you did not intentionally create this situation in order to avoid the search warrant requirement. You may not continue to search once the threat

SEARCH WARRANT EXCEPTIONS/117

of destruction has been neutralized (you may, of course, still seize evidence or contraband which inadvertently comes into your view while you are lawfully preventing destruction of other evidence).

EXAMPLES

SITUATION: *You receive information from an untested informant that a bookmaking operation is being run in the rear of a barbecue place. In order to make corroborating observations to support your request for a search warrant, you go to the area and take up a place of concealment behind the cafe. You see people going in and out the back door, counting money and putting slips of paper in their wallets. One bettor on his way out the back door spots you in your hiding place, starts running back inside, and yells: "The cops!" You run into the back room, detain everyone present, and seize all the visible evidence of the bookmaking setup. You also search and seize evidence from the areas within arm's reach where those present could dispose of evidence.*

RESULT: *It was reasonable to infer that once your presence was discovered, the bookies would quickly destroy evidence of their crimes. This situation would not permit you to seek a warrant. Your warrantless entry and seizure of the evidence to prevent its imminent destruction will be upheld. The evidence is admissible. (As you now know,* *other exceptions—such as officer protection and search incident to lawful arrest—will also permit you to search persons, clothing and arm's reach areas.)*

* * *

SITUATION: *You suspect that heroin is being cut and repackaged inside a mobile home. You position an officer at the bathroom window with a pack set radio and arrange a signal which she will send you if the suspect runs into the bathroom with the heroin. You then go to the front door, in uniform, without a search warrant, knock, and loudly proclaim: "Sheriff's officers! Open up!" The suspect picks up the dope and heads for the bathroom. You get the signal, bust in, and retrieve some of the dope from the flushing toilet.*

RESULT: *You intentionally created this "imminent destruction of evidence" situation. You cannot use the exception in this manner to circumvent the warrant requirement. The heroin is inadmissible.*

* * *

SITUATION: *You are dispatched to a fatal traffic collision. Witnesses point out the surviving driver, who appears to be under the influence of alcohol, and maybe of drugs. Your investigation indicates* this driver was speeding and ran a stop sign. You arrest him for vehicular manslaughter or felony drunk driving (depending on your statutes). He refuses to submit to a blood test for alcohol and drug screening. You call a medical technician and restrain the suspect while a blood sample is withdrawn.

RESULT: *In the absence of a statute prohibiting this procedure, your warrantless seizure of the blood sample is valid in order to prevent the imminent destruction of evidence (and probably also as a search incident to lawful arrest). Blood alcohol and most drugs tend to dissipate through metabolism, absorption or elimination with the passage of only a few hours. This does not permit you to obtain a search warrant. The evidence is admissible.*

LOCAL RULE:_____

* * *

SITUATION: *A reliable informant gives you the address of a building where, he tells you, there is a whole warehouse full of stolen auto parts. You go there and look through the window and see row after row of new and used auto parts. You send your partner to the courthouse for a search warrant, while you continue watching the warehouse. Your presence is discovered, so you rush into the* warehouse with supporting officers to seize custody of the auto parts.

RESULT: *Unlike the bookmaking example, this fact situation does not justify a warrantless entry to prevent the imminent destruction of evidence. The evidence in this case is too great in quantity, weight and size to be moved quickly or easily, and it is too durable in composition to be easily destroyed. In spite of the fact that your presence was discovered, there is no reasonable likelihood that destruction of this evidence is* **imminent.** *You cannot rely on this exception to validate your warrantless entry. On discovery, you should have surrounded and secured the warehouse while awaiting arrival of the search warrant. (We will discuss in Chapter 7 some principles which could still save this case.)*

BORDER INSPECTION

Coast Guard, customs officers, border patrol officers, and other officials of the Immigration and Naturalization Service and the Treasury Department have increased search-and-seizure powers over persons and property coming into the country. These searches are of little concern to most city, county and state officers, and federal regulations and operational directives closely govern the procedures which these officials are to follow.

For most officers, it is important simply to be aware that these federal officers have inspection powers that are less restricted than those of local officers; therefore, if you get word of incoming contraband, you should get in touch with the FBI, DEA, BATF, or other appropriate agency. It will usually be easier for these officers to make a warrantless inspection at the point of entry than for you to wait for the suspect to come within your jurisdiction where stricter search-and-seizure rules apply.

PAROLE AND PROBATION CONDITION

Judges and parole boards may specify that as a condition of probation or parole, the convicted person must agree to submit his person and property to warrantless search by an officer on demand. Such a condition is often very useful to the PO in making unannounced, warrantless entries, searches and seizures. It is rarely ever useful, however, to the general enforcement officer, who can't normally be expected to keep track of which criminals are "on search and seizure," and which are not. Unless this information is readily available (by computer or from an accessible PO), the field officer will not often have the chance to rely on this exception.

Before you attempt to use this exception for a warrantless entry, search, or seizure, you must know of the *existence* and the *terms* of the parole or probation search condition. You can't search someone, and then find out he's on search and seizure, and use this condition retroactively to justify your search. Depending on the terms of the probation or parole, you may have to be accompanied by the PO when you search the criminal, or the PO himself may have to make the search; the condition may only apply to the *person* of the probationer/parolee, or extend to his vehicle, or to a residence or business establishment under his control; it may be limited to daytime searches only; it may be limited by frequency (once a week), or by location (public places only).

Because of the problems of determining, in advance, the existence and terms of a parole/probation search-and-seizure condition, and because the very judges who set these conditions are often reluctant to allow you to make routine use of them, you should not expect that any significant proportion of your warrantless searches will fall under this exception.

If your local jurisdiction has a consistently-applied policy of informing you of local criminals who are placed on standard search-and-seizure terms, and of permitting you to take full advantage of this exception, this may then be a comparatively useful exception for your department.

LOCAL RULE: _____

_____
_____
_____

* * *

CONSENT

You may make a warrantless entry, search, or seizure when you have the voluntary, knowing consent of a person who has authority to grant that consent. The scope of your search is limited by the scope of the authorized consent.

Consent is not *voluntary* if it is obtained by means of expressed or implied threats, or if it merely amounts to a peaceful submission to authority.

Consent is not *knowing* if the person who gives it does not understand the consequences of his consent. In some states, the law requires you to advise a person of his *right to refuse* to consent, or requires you to obtain a *written* waiver and consent.

LOCAL RULE:_____

_____

_____

What if a person appears to you to have authority to give consent, and you rely on that apparent authority, then later find that he was *not* authorized to consent? There are decisions going both ways on the question of apparent authority: some courts have held it invalid, on the basis that a person cannot waive what he does not have; other courts have upheld it, on the basis that no deterrence of improper police conduct is furthered by invalidating consent given with apparent authority.

LOCAL RULE: _____
_____
_____
_____

The general rules on authority to consent are as follows:

1. *Husband-Wife.* Either spouse can consent to a search of shared premises, but not to legally separate property (wife can't consent to search of husband's company car, for example).

2. *Parent-Child.* A child cannot usually give valid consent for the search of his parents' property. A parent can usually give valid consent for the search of his resident child's property. There are exceptions to both of these rules.

3. *School Official-Student.* A teacher, principal or other school official who retains the combination to the student's locker can consent to a search of the locker. Since the student does not have exclusive control over the locker, he does not have an absolute right to privacy.

4. *Landlord-Tenant.* A landlord cannot consent to the search of a paying tenant's premises.

5. *Roommates.* One person can consent to the search of *commonly-shared* portions of the premises, but not to his roommate's *personal* rooms, furniture or effects.

6. *Host-Guest.* The host can consent to a search of his non-paying guest's room, but not to closed personal effects (luggage, jewelry box).

7. *Employer-Employee.* An employer can consent to a search of his employee's work area, but not of the employee's desk drawers, locker, or personal tool box. An employee can only consent to a search of his employer's premises if he is in charge of the premises during a substantial period of time (manager, superintendent, director).

As a general guideline to help you keep these rules straight, remember that any adult who normally has regular, unrestricted access to a place can usually grant consent for a search of that place, but not for a search of personal places of storage of another.

* * *

A person who validly consents to your entry or search or seizure can limit the areas of your search, and can revoke his consent at anytime, at will. If you are relying on the consent exception, you must abide by any such limitations or revocation.

EXAMPLES

SITUATION: *You lawfully arrest a murder suspect in his apartment. A homicide detective arrives on the scene and sees a small locked trunk at the end of the bed. He asks the suspect for the key. The suspect says there is no key. The detective says: "I'll get a search warrant and break it open. You might as well give me the key and save the trouble." The suspect retrieves a hidden key and hands it to the detective, who then finds a gun inside, which he seizes.*

RESULT: *The threat to get a warrant and break into the trunk makes the suspect's consent involuntary. The gun is inadmissible.*

* * *

SITUATION: *As you are walking through a restaurant parking lot, you see a known dope dealer sitting on the hood of a parked car, talking to a woman. You walk up and ask him if he minds if you search him. He says: "I don't guess I have any choice." You search him and find narcotics.*

RESULT: *This is not a voluntary consent, but a peaceful submission to authority. The evidence is inadmissible.*

* * *

SEARCH WARRANT EXCEPTIONS/127

SITUATION: *You learn that Louie, a juvenile thief, has just stored a stolen motorcycle in his parents' garage. The source of your information is inadequate for a search warrant. You go to Louie's home and talk to his mother at the front door. You tell her you'd like to look in the garage for a stolen motorcycle, that she can refuse to consent to your search if she wishes, and that if you find the stolen motorcycle, it will mean Louie's arrest and prosecution. She says: "If Louie's doing these things, I want to know about it. I don't want any stolen motorcycle in my garage. Come on—we'll both go look." She signs a written form for consent to search. You seize the motorcycle from the garage.*

RESULT: *This was a valid, voluntary consent. The evidence is admissible.*

* * *

Consent is a <u>last-resort basis</u> for searching or gaining entry. It is normally used only where you lack sufficient PC for a warrant or an arrest, and no other exception applies. It is <u>the most difficult exception to prove in court</u>, because those who give consent and later see the negative consequences to themselves or their friends or family members, have a predictable habit of telling the judge they did *not* consent, or did not do so knowingly, or consented only out of fear of the armed officers confronting them, or were threatened or given some promissory inducement, or attempted to revoke or limit the consent and you failed to honor such attempt. And there is always the potential problem of apparent authority turning out to be inadequate. Because the prosecution has the burden of proving valid consent, and because your claim of consent will almost always be disputed by the defendant in court, you should never rely on consent as the solitary basis for a warrantless entry, search, or seizure, unless you simply have no other choice. If you are forced to rely on consent, try to get it in writing, or have as many officers or citizens as possible witness your request and the person's grant of consent.

PRIVATE ACTION

The exclusionary rule applies only to governmental actions. If a private person, such as a merchant, a crime victim, a witness, a doctor, or a UPS shipping clerk, becomes suspicious and conducts a warrantless search or seizure and then turns evidence over to you, there is no 4th Amendment problem. This rule does not apply, however, if the private person is working in cooperation with governmental officers in an investigation, since he would thereby become an agent of the government.

NON-SEARCHES

There are some legitimate law enforcement activities which may sometimes *incidentally* produce

SAMPLE FORM

CONSENT TO SEARCH

I, *Bradley Thomas,* have been informed of and fully understand my constitutional right not to have my person or property searched without a search warrant. I understand my right to refuse to consent to such a search, and that any evidence seized will be used in criminal court.

With these rights in mind, I hereby consent to allow *Officers D. Davenport and L. Burton* of the *Dearborn, Michigan Police Department* to conduct a complete search, without a warrant, of *my person, my vehicle (1965 Chevrolet, Michigan license T634 TY), and my residence at 44 Lawton Lane, Apartment 10-B, Dearborn, Michigan, including all places within my vehicle and within my apartment.*

I also authorize these officers and any other officers summoned by them to take from *my person, vehicle and apartment* any papers and property which they desire.

I give this consent freely and voluntarily, without reservation. I have not been threatened, or given any promise, to induce this consent. My consent is not a mere submission to the authority of armed officers, but is my own personal choice.

Signed: *Bradley Thomas*   Witness: *Lou Burton*
Date: *August 12, 1980*   Witness: *Dan Davenport*
Place: *44 Lawton Lane*   Witness: *Beth Hughes*
Dearborn, Michigan

evidence, but which are not really searches. The 4th Amendment does not apply to activities which are not searches or seizures.

At time of *booking,* you may conduct a standard *inventory* inspection of the arrestee's clothing and personal property. The object of the booking inventory is not the discovery of evidence, but the proper safeguarding and accounting of the arrestee's possessions while he is in custody. If a standard booking inspection and inventory produces evidence, you may seize that evidence and use it against the arrestee. *However,* if the arrestee is carrying a locked container, your storage of which will not present any safety or accountability problems, you should list it on the inventory as "1 locked zipper money bag with initials JLH." Going inside this container would probably be viewed by most courts as a search, rather than an inventory.

To be sure your booking inventories are properly regarded by the courts, they should be uniform in every way: always performed at the jail (not in the field); always performed by the arresting officer, or the booking officer, or the property custodian (not by follow-up investigators); always listing inventoried items on a standard form; and keeping inventoried property in a separate place from seized property (not in the evidence locker).

A few jurisdictions will permit an "accelerated booking inspection" in the field.

Some jurisdictions (Texas and Louisiana, for example) may require that before any inventory, you first ask the arrestee if he wants to make other arrangements for the disposition of his personal property, or if he wants to waive any claims arising from the loss or destruction of his property while he is in custody; failure to extend these options to an arrestee may result in suppression of evidence discovered in the inventory.

LOCAL RULE:_____
_____
_____
_____

When an automobile is to be towed or impounded (e.g., as evidence, to remove a traffic hazard, due to parking violations, or following a collision), you may conduct a standard inventory inspection for the protection of the owner and your department. The same guidelines apply as for booking inventories (including the Louisiana-type restriction in a few jurisdictions).

In *Colorado v. Bertine,* the U.S. Supreme Court ruled that an automobile inventory can lawfully include the contents of all compartments and containers in the vehicle—whether open or closed—but only if the department's standardized procedure makes such inspection mandatory in every such case. If the scope of the inventory is left to the discretion of the individual officer, this exception will not apply.

In a few jurisdictions, your automobile inventory inspection is limited to the passenger compartment and glove compartment, and a warrant is required to get into the trunk.

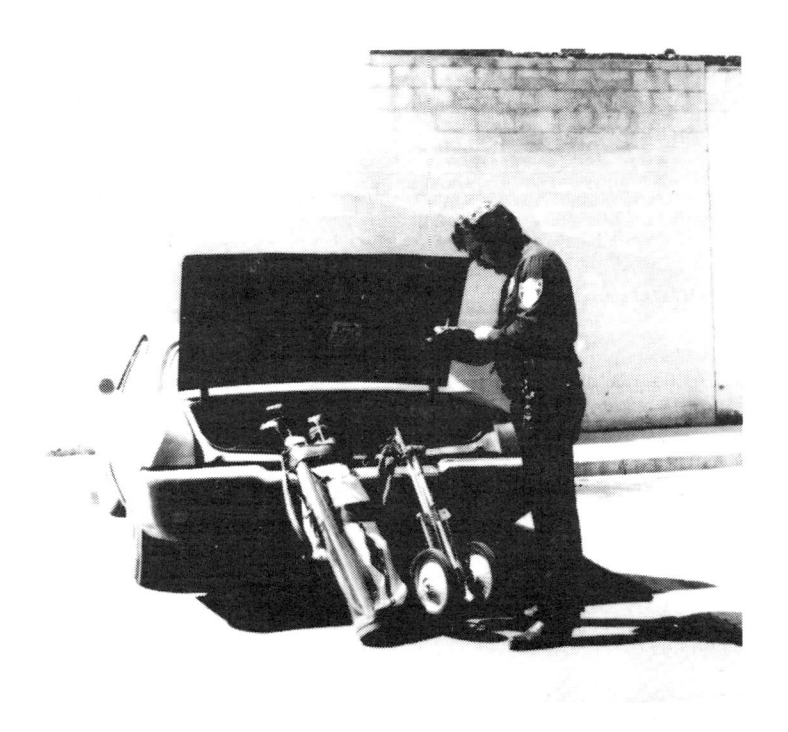

INVENTORY

An inventory is not a search. Don't treat it like one, and maybe the courts won't be too quick to accuse you of using an inventory inspection as a pretext for an unlawful search.

LOCAL RULE:⎯⎯⎯⎯⎯⎯⎯⎯⎯⎯⎯⎯⎯⎯⎯⎯⎯⎯⎯

⎯⎯⎯⎯⎯⎯⎯⎯⎯⎯⎯⎯⎯⎯⎯⎯⎯⎯⎯⎯⎯⎯⎯⎯⎯⎯⎯⎯⎯⎯⎯⎯
⎯⎯⎯⎯⎯⎯⎯⎯⎯⎯⎯⎯⎯⎯⎯⎯⎯⎯⎯⎯⎯⎯⎯⎯⎯⎯⎯⎯⎯⎯⎯⎯

When you have lawfully arrested a suspect, you may require him to submit to mugging and printing, to appear in a lineup (counsel must be provided and notified if the suspect has been formally charged), to try on clothes, masks, or disguises related to the crime, to give a handwriting exemplar, to give a voice sample (non-incriminating statements or words only), or to give samples of his hair, saliva, breath, urine, blood, footprints, or teeth impressions (procedures used to obtain these samples must not be "shocking").

Even if your arrest is eventually declared unlawful, the Supreme Court has held that non-evidentiary items may still be admitted (e.g., fingerprints, witness identifications of the suspect's face).

PRETEXTS

I don't have to tell you that since 1965, many judges have regularly expressed in their written opinions an almost-obsessive suspicion of police activity in the search-and-seizure area. They apply the warrantless exceptions very narrowly, and they closely examine your every move to see whether you were exploiting some pretext in order to get around their strict search-and-seizure rules. Whatever you do, don't feed these suspicions by walking into court with a search and seizure that smells of pretext. If you do that just once, you may never win another suppression hearing before that judge again.

EXAMPLES

SITUATION: *You are assigned to plainclothes narcotics investigation, driving an unmarked car. You roll by Danny the Dealer's house to see what the action is, and you see a car just pulling away from the curb. You recognize the driver as a local hype, and there's no doubt in your mind that he just made a buy at Danny's and will be holding at least a dime bag.*

You follow his car for a few blocks and notice that his brake lights never come on when he stops. He also seems to be doing a little weaving and is driving only 20 in a 45 zone. Although you suspect that he's driving cautiously because he's burned you, the slow driving and slight weaving **could** *mean he's DWI. And anyway, he's supposed to have working brake lights. You stop him.*

You tell him you stopped him because of brake lights, and also because you want to give him a field sobriety test. He gets out, and you go through the motions of the FST. During this time, you've seen symptoms of heroin influence in his appearance and reactions. You arrest him for being under the influence of an opiate. Incident to the arrest, you search him and find heroin.

At the station, you check his eyes and determine that he's not sufficiently under the influence for a good case on that charge. You book him for possession.

Your activity logs for the past 90 days would show that you have not written a single traffic citation, you have not logged a single warning for defective equipment, and you have not made a single arrest for DWI. You do not carry a citation book in the field.

RESULT: *Almost any court will throw out your possession case. You used traffic-related pretexts to allow you to stop the car, contact the driver, and get him out where you could gain observation of his heroin symptoms, which in turn led to a search and a "poison tree" seizure. Nothing in your recent activity pattern or your actions in this particular case suggests that you were seriously concerned about traffic law enforcement when you stopped the hype. Judicial opinion holds that a pretext search is an unreasonable search. The evidence is inadmissible. (Oregon courts will permit a bona fide traffic stop, even though you want to investigate another crime.)*

* * *

136/SEARCH & SEIZURE HANDBOOK

SITUATION: *You are on uniformed patrol in a marked car. One of your regular duties is traffic law enforcement. You carry a citation book in your car and have recently and regularly issued citations. You see Freddy the Fence driving along. You know that whenever he has been stopped, he's had stolen property in the car.*

You see Freddy make an unsafe lane change. You pull him over. You go up to his window and he says: "Hey, look. I'm in a hurry, OK?" You start asking questions ("Where are you going?" "Where are you coming from?") As you talk, a coat slides off the front passenger seat into the floor, revealing an expensive camera. Freddy says: "That's mine! I was just taking it to get fixed." You ask him some questions about lenses, shutter speed, and apertures, and his answers show that he doesn't know anything at all about the camera. You properly investigate further, and eventually arrest Freddy for receiving stolen property.

You do not issue a citation for the unsafe lane change. You did not carry your citation book when you got out and walked up to Freddy's window. You never discussed the lane change with Freddy.

RESULT: *Since you did not follow through on your supposed reason for stopping Freddy, and your* *actions and omissions clearly showed you had no intention of pursuing the matter of the traffic violation once you had used it to stop Freddy's car, you are guilty of exploiting a pretext to try to circumvent search-and-seizure restrictions. The camera, Freddy's statements about it, and your observations are all inadmissible.*

TACTIC: *If you intend to use a traffic violation as your PC to stop a car or a pedestrian, treat the situation like a traffic stop: carry a citation book, use it regularly, take it with you to the stopped car, discuss the violation with the driver, and <u>issue the citation</u>—even if you ultimately arrest the driver for mass murder. If you fail to follow through, you create a substantial risk that a suspicious judge will throw out anything you find—from a couple of joints to a carload of dead bodies—on a finding that you unlawfully exploited a pretext for the search or seizure.*

* * *

We've covered a lot of ground in this chapter and the last, but since the great majority of your searches and seizures will be *warrantless*, it was important to focus more attention in this area. As a summary, you can use the checklist of the rules and exceptions in Chapter 8.

If a person has a reasonable expectation of privacy in the place where you want to search, and if none of the exceptions for warrantless search apply, you must obtain a search warrant, as we discuss next in Part Three. □

NOTES ON LOCAL RULES

PART THREE

THE SEARCH WARRANT

5

GETTING THE WARRANT

Let's face it—cops hate to mess with search warrants. It's a genuine hassle. It's inconvenient. It's time-consuming. And some cops think it's downright demeaning for a grown, professional lawman to have to go get a "note from Mama" before he can do his job. Just when you're hot on the trail and you want to swoop down on some hood and round up all the evidence while you know it's still there, you have to put your detective impulses into neutral, sit down at a typewriter and fill out a bunch of forms, and then go over to the courthouse and cool your heels until you can get a judge to spare you a few minutes of his valuable time. And if you've made a mistake or left something out in all the paperwork, you have to start all over. In the meantime, you just *know* that sneaky little crook has found out that you've found out, and he's disposing of all the evidence. No doubt about it, it's a hassle.

But let's face it—the Constitution and the courts make search warrants absolutely necessary if you don't have one of the exceptional cases we've talked about. There's no point in getting impatient and doing your swooping and seizing *without* the warrant if the prosecutor is going to refuse to prosecute the case once he sees your search-and-seizure violation. You don't accomplish anything by trying to ignore the search warrant requirement, except perhaps to grant the crook immunity from prosecution.

So as unnatural and inconvenient as it may be to get and use search warrants, the best thing you can do is face the fact that it's a reality of proper law enforcement work. In the end, you'll save yourself a lot of problems and frustration if you just accept that fact and learn to accommodate yourself to it. And you'll be a far more effective law enforcement officer when you've mastered the mechanics of assembling and executing search warrants. As with anything else, the more often you use the search warrant as a tool of your trade, the more comfortable and proficient you will become with it. (And personally, I think that the more often officers force judges to miss lunch to work on warrants, or to have to stay late in the afternoons, or to be awakened in the middle of the night, the sooner the courts will adopt a more practical approach to warrantless searches.)

Search warrants give us a big advantage in the prosecution of cases: whereas warrantless searches are presumed unreasonable, with the burden on the prosecution to prove otherwise, searches conducted under a warrant are presumed *valid*, and the *defense* has the burden of proving otherwise. This means that if you spend a few extra hours to get a warrant, you'll probably *save* a few extra hours later on by not having to go to a suppression hearing. Use of the warrant also means you're far more likely to save the *evidence* (and often, the *conviction*, too).

So if we're agreed on the advisability of obtaining search warrants whenever possible, here is the basic information you need to know.

WHAT IS A SEARCH WARRANT?

A search warrant is a written order, signed by a magistrate, directed to a law officer, commanding him to search a specified place for specified personal property, and to bring it before the magistrate if found.

OBJECTS OF A SEARCH WARRANT

In the federal jurisdiction, a warrant can be issued for any property constituting evidence of a federal crime.

State statutes spell out clearly the categories of property for which warrants can be issued. Usually, warrants will issue for *stolen* or *embezzled* property, for *fruits, instrumentalities* or other *evidence* of a past felony or any planned future crime, or for evidence which will help establish the *identification* of the perpetrator of a committed felony.

Before you go to the trouble of filling out all the paperwork for a search warrant, check your statutes to be sure that the property you want to seize is a lawful object for a search warrant in your state. If in doubt, consult your legal advisor or prosecuting attorney.

LOCAL RULE: _____

_____

_____

FORM OF THE WARRANT

There are 3 major components of the search warrant "paperwork:" the *warrant* itself, the *affidavit* in support of the warrant, and the *return* of seized items. In many jurisdictions, the prosecutor will insist on approving your paperwork before you go to the judge (to check it for completeness and compliance with local statutes). Often, the prosecutor will actively assist you in preparing the various forms. In some jurisdictions, the prosecutor may have neither the time nor the desire to get involved at this stage and will leave

GETTING THE WARRANT/145

you on your own. Check with your supervisor or prosecutor to see what the local policy is on this.

LOCAL RULE:_____

Statutes specify items of information which must appear in a warrant (such as grounds for issuance, description of persons or places to be searched and property to be seized, the signature of the issuing magistrate, the date of issuance, and time limits for service and return). *Search warrants which omit a single required item have been held to be invalid (and the evidence suppressed).* Therefore, if you use a standard search warrant form, be sure to fill in *all* the applicable blanks; if you make up each warrant as you go, be sure to include *all* the information required by your statute.

SWEARING OUT THE WARRANT

You will recall that during our disassembly of the 4th Amendment, you learned that a warrant cannot be issued unless the probable cause for it is "supported by Oath or affirmation." There are 3 standard ways for you to give this sworn information on your PC for the warrant: *in a written affidavit, in person* before the magistrate, and *by telephone* call to the magistrate.

Telephonic search warrants are now authorized in most jurisdictions. Procedure for them is outlined in local statutes. Common features are that you call the magistrate on a tape-recorded conference call (test the tape to be sure it's working), identify yourself, have the judge identify himself, ask the judge to administer the oath to you over the telephone, read a completed warrant and affidavit to the judge, and ask him to authorize his signature to the warrant and to state the date and time of issuance. At the earliest opportunity, a transcription of the tape is made, certified by the judge, and filed with the court clerk.

Telephonic warrants are usually sought during times when the court is closed, or when the nearest judge is several hours away and circumstances won't allow you to drive over to his location. You should generally *not* use a telephonic warrant if you have a choice, due to the inherent technical problems that can develop with telephone lines and tape recorders.

Check to see if local statutes and policies permit telephonic search warrants, and under what circumstances. If they *are* authorized, ask for a checklist or a sample script to keep in your briefcase for use when the situation suddenly arises.

LOCAL RULE:_____

_____

_____

You would normally use the technique of appearing *in person* before the magistrate to give sworn oral testimony in support of the warrant only when time is critical. The disadvantage of using this technique is that it doesn't allow you to check over your statements in advance, to be sure you haven't left anything out (as you can easily do with a written affidavit). If you *do* give an oral affidavit, be sure you take an oath *before* you begin. (If you forget, go back and start over. In a case where the officer was getting a *telephonic* warrant and took an oath in the middle of his testimony that "the testimony you shall give and have already given is the truth . . . ," the appellate court invalidated the warrant.) Your oral affidavit must be transcribed by an official court reporter, and promptly certified and filed.

Because of its advantages, the *written affidavit* is the most common means of setting out sworn PC for a warrant. You can put into it and leave out of it just what you want to. You can review it before submission. The prosecutor can check it over beforehand and recommend deletions or additions. In other words, you have the opportunity to get it *right* before you take it to the judge. And you don't have any recording or transcription problems. Unless logistics or emergency circumstances prohibit, you should generally use the written affidavit as your *preferred* method of supporting a request for a warrant.

CONTENTS OF THE AFFIDAVIT

Whether your affidavit is written or oral (in person or telephonic), the contents are the same. Your statutes may require something more, but the following items are always necessary.

DESCRIPTION OF PERSON OR PLACE TO BE SEARCHED

This is one of the descriptions that you have to give "with particularity." Describe the person, place or vehicle in sufficient detail that any officer serving the warrant will be sure to search the right target. When the target is a *person,* include everything you know about his description, including name, aliases, sex, race, age, height, weight, eye color, hair color and style, eye glasses, hearing aids, beards, mustaches, deformities, tatoos, habitual jewelry, habitual dress and mannerisms, and other unusual or characteristic features or traits, and the vehicle or location where he is likely to be found, together with the time, if known.

EXAMPLES

> . . . *the person of Ronald Alton Anderson, AKA "Shorty," male caucasian, approximately 35 years, 5'5", 130 lbs., blue eyes, thin/short/balding brown hair, Fu Manchu mustache, small gold earring in right ear, believed to be residing at 801 Wilson, Apartment 2, Orange, California, believed to drive a black over white 1965 Ford Mustang convertible, California license TYL661, frequently seen at the Jack-in-the-Box restaurant at 4th and Daisy in Orange around midnight.*

* * *

GETTING THE WARRANT/149

... *the person of Maria Delgado, AKA "Mary," female Mexican, 22 years, 5'2", 120 lbs., brown eyes, straight/shoulder−length/brown hair, one gold tooth (lower), usually smoking a dark brown "Cigarillo," wears large quantities of costume jewelry (bracelets and necklaces), tatoo "MD+LR" on back of right hand, believed to be within the premises described above.*

This second example is for someone you expect to find inside the building for which you are obtaining a search warrant.

When the target is a *vehicle,* include the color, year, make, model, license number, and probable location.

EXAMPLES

... *a dark green, 1978 Cadillac Seville, 4-door sedan, Oklahoma license plate No. ST 9133, spoke wheels, white sidewall tires, dented left front fender, light green interior, believed to be parked at or near 2740 N.E. 25th Street, Oklahoma City.*

* * *

... *an off-white, older model Volkswagen van, 3-door, with 2 parallel blue stripes across the front, blackwall tires, right front tire has raised white lettering which says "HUGGER," New York license plate AL 2770, believed to be parked at* or near the Trailways bus depot in downtown Albany, New York.

If the place to be searched is a residence, be sure your description shows whether it is a house, part of a house, a duplex (triplex, etc.), an apartment, a hotel/motel room, a mobile home, a cabin, or whatever else it may be. Include all the places where you want to search.

EXAMPLES

. . . *the premises at 1102 South Beaver Street, Ft. Worth, Texas, and all rooms, attics, basements, cellars, storage areas, trash containers, garages and outbuildings located on these premises, and all parts within these places. The principal building at this location is a white stucco, 2-story, single-family residential house, with dark green shingles and green shutters and window trim. It is the first house on the southwest corner of the intersection of Beaver and Cherry Streets, and the yard is enclosed with a 3-to-4-foot high white picket fence. The numbers "1102" are affixed to the front of the house on a porch column to the right of the front door as you face the house.*

* * *

. . . *the house, attic, cellar, garage, barn, silo, and all outbuildings and sheds located within 500 feet of the house, and all parts within these places, located approximately 6½ miles west of Cemetery Road on FM118, situated on the south side of the road, in Ripley County, Indiana, west of Versailles. The house is a 2-story, single-family dwelling, white with brown shingles and yellow trim. It has a raised, concrete front porch with a yellow porch swing at the east end. There is a mailbox on a pole at the edge of the road in front of the house bearing the words "LD PRYOR." An unpainted, corrugated metal barn, with a "rooster" weather vane on top, sits approximately 150 feet to the southeast of the main house.*

* * *

. . . *the premises known as 3180 Van Nuys Boulevard, apartment 218, Van Nuys, California. This unit is in a used-brick, 3-story, multiple apartment building, which has the words "Villa Linda" in large letters on the west face. Apartment 218 is on the second floor, on the left (north) side of the hallway, the third apartment from the east end. Gold-colored metal numerals "218" are attached to the apartment entry door. The premises to be searched include all rooms, attics and other parts of this apartment, and all garages, carports, storage areas and trash containers designated for the use of apartment 218.*

Follow these same examples for commercial buildings and offices, making appropriate changes. If the target location is a repository of privileged communications (doctors' and lawyers' offices, for example), be sure your description so states. Clear these with your legal advisor or prosecutor before service.

DESCRIPTION OF PROPERTY TO BE SEIZED

If you don't describe "with particularity" the things you want to seize, the search warrant may later be held to be a general, exploratory warrant, which will be invalid. Don't try to make your warrant so broad that it will cover anything you happen to come across during your search—overbroad warrants are invalid. Limit your enumeration to those things that you have PC to believe you will find.

Be as specific as possible. Don't say "narcotics and dangerous drugs" when you expect to find heroin and seconal—say "heroin and seconal." Don't say "stolen property" when you know you're looking for a portable Zenith 19" color TV set, serial number 262577511. Don't say "illegal weapons" when you know you're looking for a sawed-off Remington 12-gauge pump shotgun and an automatic Colt AR-15 rifle. If you have PC to believe that specific items will be found in your search, specify what those items are.

In addition to the primary objects of your search, you will normally want to seize other items which are normally associated with the particular crime you're investigating, and you'll want to seize things which tend to establish a connection between the evidentiary items and the person who has apparent possession and control over them. For instance, if you're searching the house of a criminal suspect, you'll want to collect some things that show who's occupying the house.

EXAMPLES

> . . . marijuana; pipes, sifters, alligator clips, baggies, and scales; utility company receipts, rent or mortgage payment receipts or coupon books, canceled mail envelopes addressed to the premises, personalized checks, and printed return-address stickers.

* * *

> . . . heroin; hypodermic needles, hypodermic syringes, eye droppers, burnt spoons, cotton, milk sugar, scales, balloons, condoms, paper bindles, rubber or plastic straps or tubes, belts, glassine envelopes, books or papers containing lists of names, addresses, dates, telephone numbers or sales transactions, and US currency; utility company receipts, rent or mortgage payment receipts or coupon books, canceled mail envelopes addressed to the premises, personalized checks, and printed return-address stickers.

OFFICER ID AND EXPERTISE

Following your description of the premises to be searched and items to be seized, you will usually identify yourself and give a detailed account of your expertise in investigating the kind of crime associated with the search warrant. Your expertise is especially important if you are going to be offering opinions within the affidavit as to the significance of some of the facts comprising the probable cause. (For instance, the expertise of a narcotics officer would be important in assessing the significance of the fact that a suspected heroin dealer was seen carrying into his house a case of powdered milk.)

Set out your ID and expertise in narrative style, in plain English, writing in the first person (some officers like to call themselves "your affiant;" however, this third-person style is awkward and unnatural—I recommend against it).

EXAMPLE

> . . . *I am a deputy sheriff with the El Paso County Sheriff's Department, and have been for the past nine years. During the last 22 months, I have been assigned to the Narcotics Division, concentrating primarily on the investigation of narcotics violations. During this time I have investigated approximately 250 narcotics cases and have arrested in excess of 100 persons for violations dealing with heroin, cocaine, PCP, marijuana, amphetamines,*

barbiturates, and other dangerous drugs. I have participated in more than 25 undercover purchases of controlled substances, and more than 65 seizures of controlled substances. I have worked with other experienced narcotics investigators and have attended more than 30 hours of classes at the Colorado Peace Officers' Academy on the subjects of identification, use, packaging and sale of controlled substances. I have qualified as an expert witness on controlled substances in both municipal and county court in excess of 20 times. I have interviewed or interrogated approximately 200 witnesses and suspects who either used or sold controlled substances. I have read and studied a total of 17 books, pamphlets and articles on the subject of drug use, symptoms, distribution, and enforcement as listed on Exhibit 1, which is attached and incorporated in this affidavit.

PROBABLE CAUSE FOR THE SEARCH

The officer requesting the warrant has to include in the affidavit a statement of his PC to believe that the sought items will be found at the place where he wants to search. This PC may come from the officer's own observations or from other sources (including hearsay from other officers, citizens, and informants). In order to justify a search warrant, the information must be *fresh, factual* and *reliable.*

If you recite facts which show that the items were at the target area last week, or even several days ago, the magistrate will probably refuse to issue a warrant. "Stale" information is not considered sufficient to establish probable cause to believe the items are still there. *You should seek a warrant as soon as possible after acquiring your PC.* If the information is already stale when you get it (for example, informant tells you he saw stolen property when he visited Freddy's house last week), you need fresh verification that the property is still there.

To insure that information within your affidavit is *factual*, you must avoid using or quoting conclusionary language, *and* you must show the *source* of any information you rely on.

EXAMPLES

> . . . *this informant told me that there were quantities of contraband in the house at 1220 S.E. 25th Street, Portland* . . .

This information is *conclusionary:* a "quantity" could be anything from one marijuana cigarette to a house full; "contraband" could be drugs, illegal weapons, stolen property, or illegal pornography. These words are not *factual*, so they will not supply PC for a search warrant.

Moreover, this statement does not show the *source* of the informant's knowledge: did he personally observe the property, or is he merely repeating an unreliable rumor? Assertions which do not reveal the source of the information are not considered factual and will not supply PC for a search warrant.

. . . this informant told me that he was inside the house at 1220 S.E. 25th Street, Portland, at about noon yesterday, August 12, 1980, and he personally saw, in the hall closet, one sawed-off shotgun, one revolver, and three canvas money sacks with the words "First National Trust Association" written on them.

See the difference? Instead of the conclusionary word "quantities," we have specific numbers; instead of the conclusionary term "contraband," we have a specific description of the things themselves. Instead of a bold assertion that the informant says the property is in the house, without some explanation of how he came by this information, we have the evidence of his personal knowledge: *". . . he personally saw . . ."*

When you're interviewing the informant, the citizen, or the fellow officer whose statements will make up part or all of your PC for a search warrant, do not accept any conclusions—ask them for detailed specifics (*"What kind of contraband?" "What kind of narcotics?" "What kind of paraphernalia?" "What kind of stolen property?" "How much?" "Where?" "When?"*). And it is also essential to establish the source of their information, by asking: *"How do you know that?"*

To insure that the information within your affidavit is *reliable,* you must show that it comes from a trustworthy source (police officer, responsible and credible citizen, tested reliable informant, police records, or other trustworthy source), *or* that the information has been corroborated by some independent means.

EXAMPLES

> . . . *I believe this informant to be reliable because he has given me information 5 times during the past 10 months which has proven to be accurate, resulting in the recovery of stolen household goods on each occasion. The most recent of these previous contacts was within the past 3 weeks.*

> . . . *I believe this citizen to be reliable because he was a witness to the robbery and voluntarily remained at the store until police arrived so that he could give a statement. He is 28 years old, works at the Carnation Dairy, and has lived within the county for the past 6 years.*

> . . . *Although the informant is untested, I believe him to be reliable because his statements were against his own penal interest, in that he was told he could be charged as an accessory and could be sentenced to 1 year in jail if convicted; he said that he understood this, and wanted to "make a clean breast of things and get right with the Lord and the law."*

> . . . *Although the informant was anonymous, I believe him to be reliable because of the following corroboration: after I received his telephone call relating the presence of the stolen car in the garage,*

I ran the license plate number through the computer and confirmed that it did in fact belong to a stolen, 1974 white Thunderbird. I called the victim and she confirmed that there was in fact a large dent in the right rear quarter panel. I phoned the suspect's next-door neighbor, John T. Hall, 2240 East 7th, Omaha, and he confirmed that the garage door had been kept closed for several days, and that he had heard "work noises, like an electric sander" during the last few evenings.

If there is no other means of establishing an informant's reliability, take him before the magistrate and have him swear to the truth of his information. The magistrate can observe his demeanor and appearance, question him about his information, and make a finding on his credibility. If you use this approach, have the magistrate make his finding *in writing* at the end of the informant's written statement; e.g., "I have examined Jake Snitch under oath and find him to be reliable. Signed, Malcolm Magistrate, August 12, 1980."

SEIZING OBSCENE MATERIAL

If you're working vice crimes and want a search warrant for films, books, magazines, photos or other forms of obscene material, you should try to obtain samples of the material and submit them to the magistrate with your warrant request. The magistrate can then make a preliminary determination that the material is obscene and is a lawful object of a search warrant.

NIGHTTIME SEARCH AUTHORITY

Most search warrants are restricted to daytime service. If special circumstances require nighttime service of the warrant (destruction of evidence, crimes committed at night, property removed by day, etc.), spell out in your affidavit what these circumstances are and why they necessitate "day or night" service of the warrant. Also, be certain that the warrant itself contains nighttime search authorization before the magistrate signs it.

PROTECTING CONFIDENTIAL INFORMANTS

Ordinarily, you need not name a confidential informant (CI) in the affidavit. If the defense claims a right to know his identity, that issue will be litigated after the warrant has already been served, and the prosecuting attorney will handle the disclosure hearing. If there is a danger that your CI will be discovered by process of elimination, it may help to refer to him in the affidavit with double pronouns, to conceal his sex: " . . . he/she personally saw marijuana . . . which was sold to him/her . . . "

You may also include a statement in your affidavit explaining why you do not want to disclose your CI's identity.

EXAMPLE

. . . I request that the identity of the informant be kept confidential. I believe that if his/her identity is made known, this would eliminate his/her future usefulness in aiding criminal investigations, and disclosure could result in injury or death to the informant from those he/she has informed on.

PHOTOGRAPHS AND DIAGRAMS

If a photograph or drawing of the person, vehicle or premises to be searched or of the property to be seized is available, you may attach it to the warrant, with a copy attached to the affidavit, and refer to it in the description paragraph: " . . . as shown in a photo marked 'Exhibit 2,' attached and incorporated in the warrant and this affidavit . . . "

CONTAINER SEARCHES

If the "place" to be searched is a closed or locked trunk, suitcase, strongbox, toolbox, jewelry box, handbag, duffel bag, laundry bag, hatbox, shoebox, or any other kind of container or compartment, prepare your affidavit and warrant according to the same guidelines as for any other place. Give a "reasonably particular" description of the target.

EXAMPLES

... *a black Samsonite attache case measuring approximately 3" x 12" x 15", with gold-colored metal initials "JLB" under the handle, now secured in the Ft. Lauderdale, Florida, Police Department evidence locker No. 44, with evidence tag attached bearing case number 80-6111.*

... *the trunk compartment, and any containers inside this trunk, of a blue 1975 Buick Riviera, Ohio license RLY 333, now parked at the Toledo Police Impound Lot at 4740 N. Broadway Street, Toledo, Ohio, with impound sticker No. 80-274 affixed to the left front windshield.*

MULTIPLE TARGETS

A single search warrant may usually be obtained for more than one person, place or vehicle. For example, if you are conducting a raid on 3 service stations suspected of dismantling stolen trucks, and provided your PC justifies a search of all 3 locations, you could list all 3 stations in 1 warrant.

LOCAL RULE:___

As a tactical matter, of course, you may want to obtain separate warrants if you need to make simultaneous service to avoid the destruction of evidence or the flight of suspects.

EXPLAINING WORDS AND PHRASES

You should avoid using street slang and technical police jargon in your affidavit. If you are required to quote an informant's use of slang, you should explain in your affidavit what the commonly-understood meaning of any such slang words or phrases is: "The term 'stomp on it,' as used by the informant, is common slang in the drug culture which means to cut or dilute the concentrated heroin by mixing it with powdered milk in order to reduce the purity of the heroin while increasing the volume of the salable mixture."

CONCLUDING STATEMENT

After you have completed your narrative statement of PC, you should conclude with a declaration of your belief that the warrant is justified.

EXAMPLE

> . . . Based upon my training and experience, and the information available to me as set forth in this affidavit and attached exhibits, I believe that the property sought will be found at the places, in the vehicle, and on the person described.

On the following pages are a sample warrant and an affidavit. Both the language of these samples and the wording of the examples used throughout this chapter should be viewed only as models. There are no "magic words" that need be or should be automatically included in your warrants and affidavits. If you need help in preparing a warrant or an affidavit, by all means consult your supervisor, your legal advisor, or your prosecutor. Always keep an extra copy of warrants and affidavits in your working documents file for future reference, but never assume that you can merely copy a previously-successful format for use in a new case which involves new facts and issues. A reference copy is for general guidance only—not a mold for all future warrants. □

NOTES

```
                Search Warrant No. 80-8-24
1                STATE OF CALIFORNIA
2                 COUNTY OF ORANGE
3                   SEARCH WARRANT
4                    PEOPLE OF THE STATE OF
5    CALIFORNIA to any sheriff, police
6    officer or other peace officer in the
7    County of Orange; PROOF by affidavit
8    having been made before me by Investi-
9    gator James Green, No. 274, Orange
10   County Sheriff's Office, that there is
11   probable cause to believe that the
12   property described herein may be found
13   at the locations set forth herein and that
14   it   was stolen or embezzled
15   you are therefore commanded to search
16   (1) the premises at 118 N. Main Street,
17   Cara Linda, California, a one-story
18   brown frame house, being the first house
19   on the northeast corner of Main and 2nd
20   Streets, enclosed by a chain-link fence
21   and identified with the numerals "118"
22   painted on the curb directly in front of
23   the house, including all rooms, attics,
24   basements, garages, outbuildings and
25   trash containers at these premises, and
26   (2) the person of Wanda May Jubal, a
27   female Negro, approximately 22 years,
28   5'4", 120 lbs., short/curly black hair,
```

1   1" scar on left thumb,
2   ///
3   for the following property: a 16" gold
4   chain with attached gold coin ring in
5   which is mounted a 1905 US $20 gold
6   coin; the letters "TRU" in the motto
7   "In God We Trust" are noticeably worn
8   down as compared with the other letters;
9   and articles of personal property tending
10 to establish the identity of the current
11 resident of the premises, including utility
12 company receipts, rent receipts, canceled
13 mail envelopes, and printed return-ad-
14 dress stickers,
15 ///
16 ///
17 and to seize it if found and bring it
18 forthwith before me, or this court, at the
19 courthouse of this court.
20   This warrant may be served <u>only be-</u>
21 <u>tween the hours of 7:00 o'clock a.m.</u>
22 <u>and 10:00 o'clock p.m.</u>
23 ///
24 Given under my hand and dated this
25 <u>12th</u> day of <u>August, 1980.</u>
26
27 Judge of the <u>Municipal</u> Court, <u>Central</u>
28 <u>Orange Judicial District.</u>

Search Warrant No. 80-8-24
STATE OF CALIFORNIA
COUNTY OF ORANGE
AFFIDAVIT FOR
SEARCH WARRANT

On the basis of my personal knowledge and information related to me as set forth below, I, Investigator James Green, No. 274, Orange County Sheriff's Office, being duly sworn, depose and say that the property described herein was stolen or embezzled

and request the issuance of a warrant to search (1) the premises at 118 N. Main Street, Cara Linda, California, a one-story brown frame house, being the first house on the northeast corner of Main and 2nd Streets, enclosed by a chain-link fence and identified with the numerals "118" painted on the curb directly in front of the house, including all rooms, attics, basements, garages, outbuildings and trash containers at these premises, and (2) the person of Wanda May Jubal, a female Negro, approximately 22 years, 5'4", 120 lbs., short/curly black hair, 1" scar on left thumb,
///

for the following property: a 16" gold chain with attached gold coin ring in which is mounted a 1905 US $20 gold coin; the letters "TRU" in the motto "In God We Trust" are noticeably worn down as compared with the other letters; and articles of personal property tending to establish the identity of the current resident of the premises, including utility company receipts, rent receipts, canceled mail envelopes, and printed return-address stickers.

    I am a deputy sheriff with the Orange County Sheriff's Office and have been so employed for the past 5 years. For the past 18 months, I have been assigned to the Investigation Bureau, working property crimes, including burglary and theft. During this time, I have made approximately 75 arrests for burglary and theft. I have conducted approximately 225 investigations into property crimes. I have participated in the recovery of stolen property approximately 115 times. I have read and studied several OCSO publications which discuss the manner in which stolen property is disposed of in Orange County.

Throughout the period of approximately the past 4 months, I have received information through official channels that Wanda May Jubal is an active "fence" of stolen property, using her home at 118 N. Main Street, Cara Linda, for both receiving and selling stolen property. This information was announced at assembly several weeks ago and has also been reported to me by investigators in our Juvenile Bureau. I have checked official records maintained by the Department of Justice in Sacramento and have learned that Wanda May Jubal has been convicted 3 times in the past 5 years on charges of receiving stolen property.

Yesterday, August 11, 1980, at about 8:30 p.m., Mrs. Louise Johnson, of 1204-A S. Baxter, Cara Linda, brought her daughter Lucy, age 15, to the station. Mrs. Johnson said that Lucy had done something wrong and wanted to tell us about it. I gave Lucy a standard Miranda advisement. She said she understood the advisement, did not want an attorney, and did want to talk to me. She told me that she babysat for

1   Mr. and Mrs. Allen Morris on the evening
2   of August 10, 1980, and stole the gold
3   coin necklace described above from
4   Mrs. Morris' jewelry box. Lucy told me
5   she had "heard around" that you could
6   get cash for jewelry from Wanda Jubal,
7   "no questions asked," at the house at
8   118 N. Main, Cara Linda. Lucy said she
9   took the necklace to that address at
10 about 6:00 p.m. yesterday, August 11,
11 1980, and sold it to a woman fitting
12 the above description who identified
13 herself as "Wanda." Lucy said she
14 received $25 cash and that when Lucy
15 left, Wanda was wearing the necklace
16 around her neck.
17   Although informant Lucy is untested,
18 I believe her to be reliable because her
19 statement was volunteered and was
20 against her penal interest, and also
21 because it was independently known
22 to officers in our department that Wanda
23 May Jubal was a suspected fence with a
24 prior record of similar activity; further, I
25 talked with Mrs. Morris by telephone
26 yesterday, August 11, 1980, at 9:20
27 p.m., and she told me that she was in
28 fact missing a gold coin necklace of the

given description, and she verified that Lucy Johnson had in fact babysat on the evening of August 10, 1980.

Based on my training and experience, and on the information known to me as set forth above, I believe that the property sought will be found at the place or on the person described.

///
///
WHEREFORE, it is prayed that a search warrant be issued.

James Green
_____
Affiant

Subscribed and sworn to before me this <u>12th</u> day of <u>August, 1980.</u>

Malcolm Magistrate
Judge of the <u>Municipal</u> Court, <u>Central</u> Orange Judicial District.

NOTES ON LOCAL RULES

6

SERVING THE WARRANT

Even though you used restraint in not rushing into a warrantless search, and even though you patiently and properly filled out the affidavit and the warrant form according to local statutes and policies, you may *still* lose the evidence (and the case) if you fail to follow proper procedure for serving the warrant. The procedure is spelled out in your state statutes, and you should consult them for specific steps, time limitations, and entry procedure. Following are common considerations in search warrant service.

WHO CAN SERVE THE WARRANT?

A warrant is an order directed to a specified group of officers; for example, " . . . to any sheriff, police officer, or other peace officer in the County of Orange . . . " It need not be served by the officer who signed the affidavit; any officer in the authorized group may serve it. Before you go out to serve a warrant, therefore, read it and make sure you fit within the authorized group.

Officers serving a search warrant should also bear in mind that whoever finds and seizes property will probably be called to testify later in court. If the primary investigator on a case plans to be the chief witness, it is advisable for him to do as much of the searching and seizing as is practical. Officers who might not be available for trial (reserves, retiring or resigning officers, those scheduled for vacation or transfers) may assist in securing the premises during the search, but they should not actively participate in the search or seizure.

JURISDICTION

If the target of a search warrant is a person, vehicle, mobile home, container, or other movable object, be sure to observe jurisdictional limitations on service of the warrant. If it calls for service within a specified county, for example, do not try to serve it in a neighboring county. Wait until the target returns to the local county, or apply to a judge within the neighboring county for a new search warrant.

SERVING THE WARRANT/175

When you go out to serve a search warrant, be sure you're among the authorized group of officers for service, observe jurisdictional and time limitations, and comply with "knock-notice" statutes.

If you keep the warrant concealed behind you as you approach the door, the occupants are less likely to guess your purpose, and more likely to answer the door.

TIME LIMITS

There are 2 kinds of time limits for service of the warrant. Unless the magistrate authorizes nighttime service, on a showing of good cause, the warrant can normally only be served during specified daytime hours. If the warrant only says "daytime service," and does not prescribe certain hours (such as 7:00 a.m. to 9:00 p.m.), you may serve it between sunrise and sunset. If you begin executing the search during daylight hours and have not finished by nightfall, you may continue with your search until completed.

The other time limitation is on the number of days from date of issuance within which you must execute service of the warrant. In the federal jurisdiction and most states, this outside limit is 10 days. *However,* the courts generally require that warrants be executed "forthwith," which means as soon as is reasonably possible. If you delay service of the warrant for a few days, you run the risk that a reviewing court will later determine that your PC became stale during this delay, and that service was not sufficiently timely (even though you were still within the 10-day limit). And, of course, the longer you delay in serving the warrant, the greater the likelihood that evidence will be disposed of. The best practice is to serve the warrant as soon as possible after you obtain it.

LOCAL RULE:_____
_____
_____

ENTRY

The manner of getting into the premises is 1 of the 2 areas where officers most frequently ruin service of the warrant. Most jurisdictions have a "knock-notice" statute which requires you to knock on the door and wait a reasonable time for someone to answer the door. If someone comes, you identify yourself and state your purpose ("Officer Dillon, United States Marshal. I have a warrant to search this house.")

If you wait a reasonable time and no one answers, you knock again and loudly identify yourself and announce your purpose. You wait a reasonable amount of time, and if you are not admitted, you may forcibly enter and execute the warrant. (Cases have held 5 seconds an insufficient time to wait, and 30 seconds a sufficient wait.)

The trouble with this scheme, of course, is that it merely provides the crook inside with a warning and a brief "grace period" during which he can flush dope down the toilet, or jack a shell into his shotgun and level it at the door as he kneels behind the couch. Therefore, whenever you have specific facts that give you probable cause to believe that compliance with the "knock-notice" statute would result in the immediate destruction of evidence or a threat to human life, you may make an unannounced entry.

You may normally use a trick or ruse to get the person to answer the door. Then, however, you must identify yourself, announce your purpose and authority, and wait to be admitted *before* you step across the threshold. If you are not in uniform, *show your badge and ID card.*

EXAMPLES

SITUATION: *Armed with a search warrant and in uniform, you knock at the door. There is no answer, but you see a man look at you through a parted curtain at a side window. You are afraid he's destroying evidence, so you break in and execute the warrant.*

RESULT: *These facts are not sufficient to show PC to believe evidence was being destroyed. Your entry was unlawful, and any evidence resulting from your search will be suppressed.*

* * *

SITUATION: *In uniform, you knock at the door to serve a search warrant on a suspected heroin dealer. No one answers, but you see a man look at you through a parted window curtain, and quickly pull his head back. You immediately knock again, identify yourself, and announce your purpose, and listen at the door. You hear yelling and running inside, and inner doors slamming. You forcibly enter and execute your warrant, after only a 10-second pause.*

RESULT: *These facts show PC to believe that evidence was in danger of imminent destruction. Your entry was lawful.*

SERVING THE WARRANT/179

SITUATION: *You obtain a search warrant, based on a woman's statement that her common-law husband has "gone crazy" and has stocked up their house with grenades and automatic rifles and is threatening to kill someone. She has moved out (can no longer consent to entry). She tells you that her husband will shoot anyone who tries to get in. You run a record check and learn that the man is an escaped mental patient with a record of violence. When you surround the house, you see through a window that the suspect is asleep on a bed, with hand grenades lying on a nightstand. You quietly enter and remove the grenades before waking the suspect and executing the warrant.*

RESULT: *Your noncompliance with the "knock-notice" law is excusable because of the apparent threat to life which existed.*

* * *

SITUATION: *Officers who tried to serve search warrants on a cocaine dealer in the past found that the suspect would yell: "I'm coming... just a minute until I get some clothes on," and would then destroy all evidence while officers stood on the porch. To serve your new warrant, you dress in a postman's uniform and knock at the door with your badge cupped in your hand. When the suspect opens the door, you display your badge and say: "Police officer with a search warrant."*

He starts to close the door and you stick your foot in the doorway, saying: "Will you let me in?" The suspect says: "No!" and turns and runs. You run in after him and stay with him while other officers enter and search, finding cocaine.

RESULT: *These facts justified your entry. The evidence is admissible.*

* * *

Officers who go to the premises with you to assist in the search do not have to enter by the same door you use. Once you have been admitted, or have lawfully entered forcibly or unannounced, assisting officers may enter through other doors.

Some states require you to comply with the "knock-notice" procedure at *inner* doors (bedrooms, kitchen, bathrooms), even after you have lawfully entered the building.

LOCAL RULE: ⎯⎯⎯⎯⎯⎯⎯⎯⎯⎯⎯⎯⎯⎯⎯⎯⎯⎯

⎯⎯⎯⎯⎯⎯⎯⎯⎯⎯⎯⎯⎯⎯⎯⎯⎯⎯⎯⎯⎯⎯⎯⎯⎯⎯⎯⎯⎯

SCOPE OF THE SEARCH

The warrant orders you to search for specific items of property. You must limit your search to places where those items could be found; you must not remain on the premises any longer than is necessary

SERVING THE WARRANT/181

to complete your search; and once you have found and seized the items, you must stop searching.

You may, however, seize any contraband which comes into your view while you are lawfully searching, whether or not it is named in the warrant. You may also seize evidence of the crime you are investigating, even though it is not listed in the warrant, if it comes into your view during your search and you have cause to believe it is related to the criminal activity under investigation.

If your warrant for *small* items includes "all places within the premises" and you find a locked suitcase in the closet, you do *not* need another warrant to open and search it. However, if your warrant is only for a *large* item (stolen motorcycle) and you find a locked suitcase, you cannot open it without a new warrant.

Persons present at the premises who are *not* listed in the warrant may be patted down for weapons for your protection. They may not be searched further unless one of the warrantless exceptions applies.

EXAMPLES

SITUATION: *You are serving a warrant for "a Smith-Corona electric typewriter, 'Coronet' model, serial number 24L111592." Inside a medicine bottle on the mantle you find and seize marijuana. While looking for the typewriter in a closet, you find and seize a nunchaku.*

SCOPE OF SEARCH

Don't search inside a kitchen cupboard if your warrant is for items too large to be concealed there. You are authorized to search only in places where there is a reasonable likelihood of finding the objects of your search warrant.

RESULT: *You could not expect to find a typewriter inside a medicine bottle; therefore, you were not permitted to look inside the medicine bottle for the typewriter, and so the marijuana is inadmissible. The closet, on the other hand, was a likely place to look for the typewriter. Since you came across the illegal weapon there, it is admissible. (Note: If you had found the marijuana in a cigar box, while looking for utility receipts or cancelled mail, it would be admissible, provided the warrant listed receipts and mail as objects of your search.)*

* * *

SITUATION: *While serving a warrant for a stolen camera, you find and seize the camera and other objects of the warrant. You then look in kitchen cupboards and find marijuana, which you also seize.*

RESULT: *Your authority to search ended when you had found the objects. You exceeded the scope of the warrant by continuing to search. The marijuana is inadmissible.*

TACTIC: *Whenever your PC will justify, always try to include a small object (rent receipt, key, etc.) in the warrant. This will allow you to search places such as desk drawers, jewelry boxes, kitchen*

INADVERTENT DISCOVERY

As long as you have not exceeded the scope of your authorized search, you may seize any contraband that comes into your view while you are executing the warrant.

A baggie of marijuana found during a lawful search for a stolen weapon is admissible.

cupboards, shoeboxes, and envelopes. Bear in mind that if you **start** *your search in the place where you are most likely to find the objects, your authority will end as soon as you discover them; if you leave the likely hiding place until* last, *you will be able to conduct a thorough search of all other possible hiding areas and seize any contraband or evidence which comes into view. Do not abuse this tactic, however, if your PC points to a* **precise** *location (informant told you which drawer the gun is kept in).*

AFTER THE SEARCH

If you find and seize property, you must leave a **copy** of the warrant and an inventory receipt for the seized items with the person in charge of the premises. Do not leave the *original* warrant. Do not leave any copies of the *affidavit.*

If you seize items from the premises while no one is home, leave a copy of the warrant and inventory receipt in a conspicuous place. Be sure the premises are secured against burglars when you leave to the same extent as when you arrived (don't drive away leaving broken windows and doors that *you* forced open).

RETURN OF THE WARRANT

Within a specified time (usually 10 days from date of issuance), you must return the original warrant and affidavit to the magistrate who issued it. If you seized property listed in the warrant, you must also file with the magistrate an itemized inventory (most jurisdictions require you to retain custody of the property pending further court order on its disposition). Do *not* include in the return inventory any items seized as contraband unrelated to the crime for which the warrant was executed. Such property was not seized pursuant to the warrant, but was taken on authority of a warrantless exception (usually, "plain view" from a place where you had a right to be).

LOCAL RULE:_____

_____

_____

Unfortunately, even if you do everything right, you may still lose the evidence if you are not adept at explaining your actions in such a way as to convince the prosecutor and the judge that you did *in fact* do everything right. And fortunately, even if you did something *wrong,* there may still be a way to save the evidence (and the case). These topics are covered in the next, final section of the book. □

PART FOUR

SAVING THE CASE

7

SALVAGING THE SEARCH AND SEIZURE

When you rely on a single justification to support your search or seizure, you've got all your eggs in one basket, with the obvious risks. If you make a warrantless search on the theory that the suspect had no reasonable expectation of privacy, you run the risk that the court may feel otherwise. If you rely on a warrantless exception, you run the risk that some single fact may make the exception questionable. And even when you rely on a warrant, you risk the possibility that the affidavit or the warrant was defective, or that a procedural error occurred during service.

Since there are no hard-and-fast absolutes in the law of search and seizure, you need to be alert to every possibility for saving the case from these risks. There are 5 case-saving devices which you should be prepared to take advantage of.

MULTIPLE BASES

If you have a choice, don't put all your eggs in one basket. Sometimes, you may be able to establish 2 or more theories on which to justify your search or seizure. If you can do this, you increase the odds that at least 1 of your theories will be upheld by the court.

EXAMPLES

SITUATION: *You have a search warrant to search a house and attached garage for a stolen U-haul trailer with a certain identifying number painted on the tailgate. As you walk from your car to the public sidewalk in front of the house, you notice that the garage door is standing open, and inside, you can clearly see the U-haul trailer with the ID number. You follow correct procedure for service of the warrant and seize the trailer.*

RESULT: *You now have 2 theories on which to justify your seizure (warrant, and contraband in plain view). If you had simply relied on "plain view" and stuck the warrant in your pocket, it is always*

MULTIPLE BASES

Don't rely on the PLAIN VIEW doctrine to seize a visible marijuana plant from inside a house — if there's no danger of imminent destruction, you need a warrant or consent to get inside a person's home.

possible that the defendant could produce relatives, friends and neighbors in court to contradict your testimony about the garage door being open when you arrived. Since the burden is on you to prove a warrantless exception, the evidence might be suppressed. Following through with the search warrant was good insurance.

* * *

SITUATION: *You make a lawful carstop and see the passenger apparently hiding something under his feet. You approach and look in, and you see what appears to be a baggie of marijuana sticking out from under a jacket on the floorboard at the passenger's feet. The windwing is open, and you smell burning marijuana. The driver comes out to meet you and tells you the passenger is a hitchhiker. The driver consents to your searching the floorboard of his car. You seize a baggie of marijuana.*

RESULT: *Although you had sufficient PC to seize the marijuana* **without** *obtaining consent, the fact that you were patient and obtained consent to search will make it far more difficult for the passenger to challenge your seizure of his marijuana.*

SALVAGING THE S&S/193

SITUATION: You make a lawful carstop in the daytime. You arrest the driver after your pat down of his outer clothing produces marijuana. Incident to the arrest, you decide to search inside his car. You open the door and see brass knuckles lying on the driver's seat. You seize this illegal weapon.

RESULT: These facts did not justify the frisk, and a frisk does not justify removal of items (marijuana) which could not possibly be a weapon. Therefore, the arrest was unlawful, and so was the search incident to it. The brass knuckles (as well as the marijuana) will be suppressed. Notice that if you had bothered to **look** inside the car **before** you opened the door, you would have seen the brass knuckles in plain view from a place where you had a right to be. If you had taken just a minute to cover yourself with this approach, the brass knuckles could have been saved as evidence, in spite of your error in assuming you could search incident to this arrest.

TACTIC: Even when you think you have all the authority you need to make a search or seizure, take advantage of every opportunity to reinforce and extend it. If you have PC to search a fleeting target, you may also be able to invoke the "plain view" exception by first <u>looking</u> wherever you have a right to look. You may also be able to obtain consent to search and thereby extend the scope of your search to places where your original PC

COVER THE BASES

BEFORE you open the car door to search, LOOK through the windows and see what's in plain view—this may add to your PC to go inside and search.

would not have justified searching. *You may, by running a routine warrant check, be able to make a lawful arrest and then search incident to the arrest, and also make inventory inspections of the person and vehicle. This, in turn, may produce additional PC to enable you to obtain a search warrant.*

<u>Be greedy.</u> Whenever the situation permits, develop and legally exploit as many different bases for your search and seizure as are practical under the circumstances.

GOOD FAITH

In limited kinds of cases, the U.S. Supreme Court has held that an objectively reasonable mistake by police officers will not result in the suppression of evidence, even though a technical violation of the Fourth Amendment may have occurred.

EXAMPLE:

SITUATION: *Believing in good faith that you have sufficient PC to support a search warrant, you compose an affidavit and submit it to the magistrate. On the basis of your information, the magistrate issues the warrant. When you serve the warrant, you seize incriminating evidence from the defendant's home. A reviewing court later finds, on closer examination of your affidavit and the warrant, that a technical error* occurred on the magistrate's part, and the court rules that the warrant should not have been issued as it was.

RESULT: *Although the magistrate committed a Fourth Amendment error, the deterrent purpose of the exclusionary rule would not be furthered by suppressing evidence that you seized in the reasonable belief that the warrant was valid. Under the "good faith" exception, the evidence is still admissible.*

* * *

The "good faith" doctrine has also been applied by the courts where an officer reasonably—but mistakenly—relies on the apparent authority of a person to give consent to a search, and where officers reasonably mistake one person for another in serving an arrest warrant, or one place for another in serving a search warrant, and where officers reasonably rely on a statute or ordinance that is later declared void or unconstitutional by the courts.

ATTENUATED TAINT

"Attenuated" means weakened or dissipated. Even though you may have committed a search-and-seizure error which "taints" your subsequent actions, intervening circumstances may dispel the taint to the

SALVAGING THE S&S / 197

extent that the chain of discovery (from your error to the seizure) is broken. When this happens, the court will admit otherwise-inadmissible evidence under the "doctrine of attenuated taint."

EXAMPLE

SITUATION: *During a carstop, you make an unlawful search and find a safe deposit box key, which you seize. Your intention is to trace the key and examine the contents of the box. However, you neglect to do so, and when you remember the key several weeks later and try to return it to the driver, his wife tells you to take the key and open her safe deposit box at the local bank and remove a stolen revolver which her husband forced her to put there several months ago. You do so.*

RESULT: *If you had followed through with your original intentions and found the stolen gun on your own, it would be the "fruit of the poisonous tree," tainted by your original, unlawful search. However, the circumstances in this situation bring into play the doctrine of attenuated taint.*
 What caused the taint to be attenuated? One thing was the **passage of time.** *The more time that elapses between the original error and the ultimate discovery, the more likely the taint will become attenuated (this doesn't mean you can merely sit on unlawfully-seized evidence for awhile and then use it).*

Another attenuating factor was the fact that you did not **exploit** *the unlawful seizure—you did nothing with the key to enable you to find evidence you were already looking for but hadn't been able to reach. The most significant attenuating factor in this example, however, was the* **intervening action** *of the suspect's wife, which broke into the chain of discovery and became more closely-related to the ultimate seizure than was the original, tainted search.*

TACTIC: *Whenever the defense seeks to relate your seizure of an item back to an earlier, unlawful search or seizure, point out the lapse of time, the good faith of your motives, your non-exploitation of the error, and any intervening circumstances which may have operated to attentuate any previous taint.*

INDEPENDENT SOURCE

The "doctrine of independent source" says that if you came by evidence following an unlawful search or seizure, but if you *had* and *used* (or might just as easily have used) another source of obtaining the evidence, which was completely unrelated to and independent of the illegal search or seizure, the evidence need not be suppressed.

SALVAGING THE S&S/199

EXAMPLE

SITUATION: *Before you made the carstop which resulted in the unlawful seizure of the safe deposit key, you had been working with an untested informant who also had legal access to the safe deposit box and had been promising to give you his own key, assuring you that there was a stolen revolver inside the box. However, the informant had been stalling, so you decided to stop the suspect's car and try to find his key.*

After your illegal seizure, your supervisor tells you to forget about using the key you seized, and to go back to work on the informant. Further dealings with the informant (who knows nothing of your unlawful seizure of a duplicate key), results in the informant giving you his key and lawful, valid consent to search the box. You do so.

RESULT: *The means of getting into the safe deposit box came to you lawfully, via an independent source, which was not connected to and did not result from your unlawful seizure. Under the "independent source doctrine," the gun is admissible.*

TACTIC: *Whenever 2 or more leads bring you to a piece of evidence, and one of those leads is determined to be tainted by an unreasonable search or seizure, point out that the remaining leads were* *independent of the taint and were sufficient on their own to lead you to the evidence.*

INEVITABLE DISCOVERY

Even if you unlawfully seized the key from the trunk of the car and then went directly to the bank and seized the stolen gun, it may *still* be admissible if there were other circumstances which would inevitably have led to discovery of the gun, regardless of the auto search.

EXAMPLE

SITUATION: *A detective who had been working residential burglaries had learned from a reliable informant of the presence of the stolen gun in the safety deposit box. This detective, who knew nothing of your auto search, was over at the courthouse getting a search warrant for the deposit box at the same time that you, knowing nothing of the detective's work, were retrieving the gun by use of your illegally-seized key. You meet the detective as you're leaving the bank and turn over the gun to him.*

RESULT: **Your** *seizure of the gun would have resulted in suppression under the exclusionary rule; however, since the detective would have inevitably discovered the gun through a lawful search, it will be admissible.*

SALVAGING THE S&S/201

TACTIC: *If the seizure of evidence is tainted by a previous, unreasonable search or seizure, point out that lawful police efforts or other subsequent circumstances would eventually have led to discovery of the evidence anyway.*

* * *

The courts narrowly limit application of the doctrines of good faith, attenuated taint, independent source, and inevitable discovery. Moreover, their coming into play to rescue a bad search or seizure is not something which you can predict or control. Therefore, you should never assume that you can go ahead with an unreasonable search or seizure and later be able to invoke one of these doctrines to save the case. These theories are to be argued only where it is subsequently discovered (or ruled) that a good-faith search or seizure was in fact unlawful. ☐

NOTES ON LOCAL RULES

8

WRITING YOUR REPORT

In **THE NEW POLICE REPORT MANUAL**, I've written at length on what I feel are the keys to writing a good investigative report. For a thorough discussion of report writing, I'll simply refer you to that book.

I think it's appropriate, though, to cover in a search-and-seizure handbook the special approach to reporting that's called for when you make a warrantless search or seizure.

SUBJECTIVE REPORTING

You get a lot of instruction during your training classes about the need for *objective* reporting. And while it's true that you have to be objective about reporting statements, descriptions and observations, you don't often hear that there's also a place for *subjective* reporting. That place follows your objective rendition of the facts—it is the place where you justify (if it isn't obvious) the action you took as a result of the objective facts.

When you start explaining in your report *why* you made an arrest, or conducted a search, or drew your weapon, or fired your weapon, or abandoned a pursuit, or struck someone with your baton, or choked someone out, you go from *objective* to *subjective* reporting. You are, in effect, saying: "On the basis of all of these facts, I came to the conclusion that my action was necessary because . . . "

If you were just a combination camera-and-tape-recorder, out there just to "take a report," objective reporting would be enough. But since you're also out there to think, to apply the law to the facts that you find, and to take appropriate investigative and enforcement action, you can't get by with just objective reporting. You have to record your subjective analysis of the objective facts.

Reporting on search and seizure (especially without a warrant, or beyond the scope of the warrant) requires such a combination of both objective and subjective reporting. You have to remember that prosecuting attorneys, judges, jurors, and anyone else who may read and rely on your report, won't usually know anything about police work. They won't see the significance of some of the facts you report, and so they won't understand (or approve of) some of your actions. You have to make these readers approach the facts from *your viewpoint*, so your actions will seem perfectly reasonable and justifiable to them. That requires subjective reporting.

EXAMPLES

OBJECTIVE REPORT: . . . *I saw that the license plate on the car read "T27551," and then I saw that a piece of red ribbon was tied to the car's radio aerial. I called for a back-up officer and stopped the car at 900 N. Laurie. When I approached the driver's window, I saw that there were 2 young Mexican men in the front seat and 2 more in the rear seat, and a Mexican girl in the rear between the 2 men. The girl had 2 small pink areas on her neck, her eye makeup was streaked on her cheeks, and her clothing was in disarray (part of her blouse was not tucked in, and several buttons were unbuttoned).*

    I asked the driver, Herrera, for his license and registration, which he gave me. The registration certificate showed the car's license number as VVY 488.

    Rios, the man seated to the girl's left, had a black sock wadded up in his left hand. There were flecks of gold paint on his fingertips and above his upper lip.

Officer Mills arrived and we ordered all of the people out of the car. I watched as Rios climbed out of the car, and I asked him to count to 10. He did so. I asked him if he had been drinking; he said that he had not.

While Officer Mills detained the 4 men near their car, I took the girl, Hilda, to the rear of my patrol car and asked her to tell me what was going on. She said: "Nothing happened. I'm not going to tell you anything."

I asked her to wait in front of my car, and I returned to where Officer Mills and the 4 men were. I arrested Herrera and Rios. I searched them and seized the black sock from Rios and 3 empty, unused plastic sandwich bags from inside Herrera's shirt. I searched their car and seized a switchblade knife and a can of gold spray paint, both of which I found under the driver's seat. I also seized a pair of stained, white panties, which I found stuffed down behind the back seat, in the area where Rios had been sitting.

I took Hilda back to the street behind my car again and told her I had found the knife and the panties, and that the only way for her to be safe now was to help us put these guys away. She began crying, and said: "They raped me. Oh, my God, they all raped me." I arrested the other 2 men, searched them, and seized a rawhide boot lace which I found in Cordova's left shirt pocket.

WRITING YOUR REPORT/207

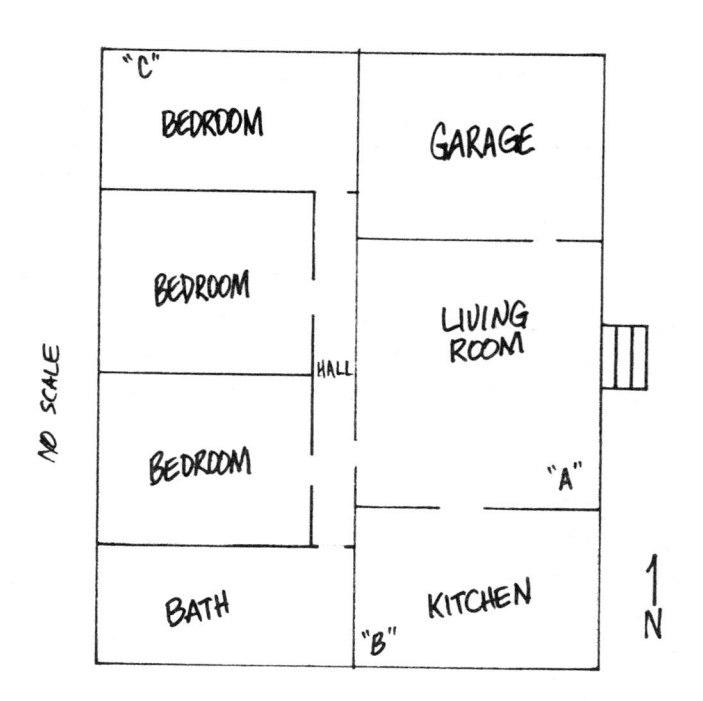

```
         "C"
      BEDROOM            GARAGE


      BEDROOM
                         LIVING
                  HALL   ROOM

                                    "A"
      BEDROOM


                                    ↑
      BATH              KITCHEN     N
                  "B"
```
NO SCALE

SKETCH OF SEARCH: 1421 MILL STREET. CI#80-2751
"A" = Location of .38 Colt in drawer, found by TILLIS.
"B" = Baggie of mj found in can, by Officer NEWTON
"C" = .38 ammo in dresser drawer, found by TILLIS.
Sketch by TILLIS, #253

Use sketches or diagrams whenever possible to show WHO found WHAT, and WHERE. A quick sketch is a far better record than several pages of narrative descriptions.

I also seized the red ribbon from the radio aerial.

As you can see, if you were to write a purely objective report such as this, without any subjective opinions, conclusions, knowledge, thoughts or suspicions, you would never get the case past your supervisor, let alone the prosecutor or the judge. This purely objective report does *not* show any PC for stopping the car, any PC for arresting Rios and Herrera, nor any PC for searching the car. It does not fully explain *why* you did what you did.

In order to give the reader the benefit of your viewpoint on these objective facts, you have to report on your continuing subjective analysis of the objective data. This is true *wherever* you report on a search-and-seizure issue. *Don't try to write a purely objective report about 4th Amendment activities.* It won't work.

As you read and compare the following combination objective/subjective version of the same carstop, notice that *all* of the additional information here is subjective in nature—things going on inside the officer's head, and not detectable by an outside, objective observer.

OBJECTIVE/SUBJECTIVE REPORT: . . . *I saw that the license plate on the car read "T 27551." I recognized this sequence (1 letter and 5 digits) as a sequence which is only assigned to trucks, and not to passenger cars (which have a sequence of 3 letters and 3 digits). I suspected that this plate didn't belong to this car—a situation which frequently* indicates that either the vehicle or the plates may be stolen, and that the driver may be using the car for unlawful activity, with false plates attached to prevent tracing and apprehension.

    I also saw that a piece of red ribbon was tied to the car's radio aerial. This made me more suspicious, because I had previously heard in street contacts and official briefings of a gang initiation ritual of "Los Hombres," a Mexican youth gang. According to the information I had, new members of "Los Hombres" had to kidnap and rape a girl under the age of 18, from the neighborhood of a rival gang. They had to bring back her panties, preferably with some blood on them, as proof of their deed, and they were to drive through the rival gang's territory afterward with a red ribbon flying from their aerial as a symbol of their rape.

    This kind of activity could explain the use of unassigned license plates on the car. I therefore called for a back-up officer and stopped the car at 900 N. Laurie. When I approached the driver's window, I saw that there were 2 young Mexican men in the front seat and 2 more in the rear seat, and a Mexican girl in the rear between the 2 men. The girl appeared to be 1 or 2 years under the age of eighteen. These observations increased my suspicion that the 4 men may have just committed a "Los Hombres" gang rape of the girl.

    The girl had 2 small pink areas on her neck. I suspected that these might have been caused by the men pressing the tip of a knife or the muzzle of a gun against her throat, or grabbing her around the throat during a kidnap or a forcible rape. I became even more suspicious when I saw that her eye makeup was streaked on her cheeks, as if from crying, and that her clothing was in disarray (part of her blouse was not tucked in, and several buttons were unbuttoned), as if from hasty or inattentive dressing.

I asked the driver, Herrera, for his license and registration, which he gave me. The registration certificate showed the car's license number as VVY 488. This confirmed my suspicion that the car was being driven with illegal plates (a booking offense), and increased even more my suspicions of a possible rape. I did not discuss the problem of the plates at this point because I did not want to prompt the suspects to flee while they still had the girl in the car with them, and I did not want them to suspect that I suspected them of anything serious. I could not tell for sure whether the right rear passenger had a weapon against the girl's side. For her safety and my own, I did not want the men to feel threatened before my back-up officer arrived.

I saw that Rios, the man seated to the girl's left, had a black sock wadded up in his left hand. There were flecks of gold paint on his fingertips and above his upper lip. I knew from my experience in arresting juvenile paint sniffers that they often spray the paint into a thick sock or a plastic sandwich bag, stick their nose and mouth into this, and inhale the fumes until they become intoxicated. This process often leaves traces of paint on their fingers and around their mouths and noses. I therefore suspected that Rios had been sniffing spray paint recently, and might be under the influence of toluene in public (a booking offense).

    Officer Mills arrived. For our safety, the safety of the girl, to avoid their sudden flight, and to permit further investigation of the 3 offenses which I suspected, we ordered all of the people out of the car. I watched as Rios climbed out of the car, and he seemed to me to be moving very slowly and with difficulty. This increased my suspicion that he might be under the influence of toluene. I asked him to count to 10, and he did so very slowly. I asked him if he had been drinking; he said that he had not. I then concluded that Rios had been inhaling, and was under the influence of, poisonous fumes.

    While Officer Mills detained the 4 men near their car, I took the girl, Hilda, to the rear of my patrol car and asked her to tell me what was going on. In a very loud voice, which I felt the suspects could overhear, she said: "Nothing happened. I'm not going to tell you anything." I believed that Hilda probably was the victim of a rape but out of fear of reprisal would not say anything, and wanted to make sure the suspects knew it.

    I asked her to wait in front of my car, and I returned to where Officer Mills and the 4 men were. I knew that the motor vehicle computer was down and could not be used to check on the truck plates. I arrested Herrera for illegal use of plates and Rios for public intoxication on poisonous fumes. I searched them and seized the black sock from Rios and 3 empty, unused plastic sandwich bags from inside Herrera's shirt. I searched their car for a paint can, other sniffing devices, and the proper license plates. I seized a switchblade knife and a can of gold spray paint, both of which I found under the driver's seat. I also seized a pair of white panties, with apparent bloodstains, which I found stuffed down behind the back seat, in the area where Rios had been sitting.

I took Hilda back to the street behind my car again and told her I had found the knife and the panties, and that the only way for her to be safe now was to help us put these guys away. She began crying, and said: "They raped me. Oh, my God, they all raped me." I arrested the other 2 men for suspicion of rape, searched them, and seized a rawhide boot lace, which I felt might have been carried to bind a kidnap-rape victim; I found this lace in Cordova's left shirt pocket. I also seized the red ribbon from the radio aerial.

* * *

See the difference your *subjectivity* makes? It fills in all the missing pieces of your PC for the carstop, the arrests, the searches, and the seizures. It always does. (Although many times, of course, the rationale for

WRITING YOUR REPORT/213

When you write a report about search and seizure activity, be sure to include all the details of your <u>subjective</u> analysis of the objective facts. You can't justify warrantless searches without showing the reader the basis of your actions—from <u>your</u> point of view.

your actions will be so obvious that no explanations will be needed.) Now that you know about the proper role of subjective reporting in saving your searches and seizures, don't listen the next time someone tries to tell you that police reports have to be kept objective. You know better.

SEARCH & SEIZURE CHECKLIST

As a quick reference when you get ready to write your report (or any other time you need it), I've outlined the highlights of the law on search and seizure in the following checklist. *Don't use this checklist as a substitute for a thorough familiarity with the principles discussed throughout the book.*

- ☐ **DOES THE 4TH AMENDMENT APPLY?**
  - ☐ Is your activity a *search?*
  - ☐ Is your activity a *seizure?*
  - ☐ Did the evidence result from a routine *inventory* inspection?

- ☐ **DOES THE SUSPECT HAVE STANDING TO OBJECT?**
  - ☐ Did you search *his* house or vehicle?
  - ☐ Did you seize *his* property?

- ☐ **DOES THE SUSPECT HAVE A REASONABLE EXPECTATION OF PRIVACY?**
  - ☐ Was the activity or property exposed to *plain*

view from a place where you had a right to be?
☐ Was the property *abandoned* by the suspect, through no unlawful conduct on your part?
☐ Was the activity or property located in *open fields?*
☐ Was the activity or property exposed in *public places?*
☐ Did your search or seizure affect a prisoner *in jail?*
☐ Did you acquire information by temporary *eavesdropping* on a carelessly-exposed conversation?
☐ Did you overhear a *phone conversation* with the express permission of one of the parties to the call?
☐ Did you use a *device,* such as a pen register, a body transmitter, binoculars, flashlight or beeper, only to aid you in already-lawful searches?
☐ Did you use a *ruse or trick* only to avoid violence and prompt action from a suspect's consciousness of guilt?

☐ IF THE SUSPECT HAS A REASONABLE EXPECTATION OF PRIVACY, IS THERE A RECOGNIZED EXCEPTION FOR A WARRANTLESS SEARCH OR SEIZURE, AND HAVE YOU CORRECTLY LIMITED THE SCOPE OF YOUR SEARCH?

- ☐ Is there a life-threatening or substantial property-threatening *emergency?* Scope of Search: Anyplace where the emergency requires you to look, and anything which comes into your view during your efforts to neutralize the emergency.
- ☐ Is prompt action required to insure *officer protection?* Scope of Search: The person and arm's reach area where a concealed weapon might be, if an object resembles a weapon; anything which comes into your view during this search.
- ☐ Is a *stop and frisk* justified with AS to suspect criminal activity? Scope of Search: Pat down of outer clothing for weapons.
- ☐ Did you search a *fleeting target,* such as a vehicle, on PC to believe that seizable items were inside, and with no opportunity to obtain a search warrant? Scope of Search: Wherever you have PC, except that removable **containers are not fleeting, and may require a warrant once they are under your control.**
- ☐ Was your search *incident to a lawful arrest?* Scope of Search: Person and arm's reach area for weapons, evidence, fruits or instrumentalities of the offense arrested for. Search must be contemporaneous in time and place with the arrest for a bookable offense.
- ☐ Did your entry result from a lawful, fresh, and close *hot pursuit* of a fleeing felon? Scope of Search: Person and arm's reach area.

- ☐ Was prompt entry or search or seizure necessary to prevent the *imminent destruction of evidence,* through no fault of your own? Scope of Search: Anyplace necessary to insure the preservation of threatened evidence, and anything which comes into your view while you are neutralizing the threat of destruction.
- ☐ Is a *border search* by a federal agent preferable to a later search within a local jurisdiction?
- ☐ Did you search on authority of a valid *condition of parole or probation?* Scope of Search: Depends on terms of condition imposed by judge or parole board.
- ☐ Did you obtain valid, voluntary, intelligent *consent* from a responsible adult who had authority to grant consent? Scope of Search: Limited to terms of consent and area over which consenting person has authority.
- ☐ Did you exploit a *pretext* in order to circumvent the search warrant requirement, thereby making your seizure of evidence invalid?

☐ **DID YOU OBTAIN A VALID SEARCH WARRANT?**
- ☐ Was your warrant directed toward lawful objects of a search warrant, such as stolen property and evidence of a felony?
- ☐ Did you *swear* to probable cause in person, by telephone, or in a written affidavit?

- ☐ Did you *describe with particularity* the *place to be searched,* so that any other officer could locate the proper target?
- ☐ Did you *describe with particularity* the *property to be seized,* so that the warrant is not overbroad?
- ☐ Did you include small items of *identification* with the property to be seized?
- ☐ Did you describe your *experience, training* and *expertise* in your affidavit, to supply a basis for your beliefs and conclusions?
- ☐ Did you recite *fresh* (not stale), *factual* (not conclusionary), and *reliable* (from trustworthy source or independently corroborated) information to establish PC for the warrant?
- ☐ Is *nighttime service* justified by your PC and authorized in the warrant?
- ☐ Did you have the judge make an *obscenity determination* after viewing samples and before issuing the warrant?
- ☐ Have you given reasons for *protection of informants* and worded your affidavit so as to preclude discovery?
- ☐ Should you attach *photos* and *diagrams* to clarify the affidavit or the warrant?
- ☐ Have you explained the meaning and significance of slang words and phrases?

☐ **DID YOU EXECUTE THE WARRANT PROPERLY?**

- [ ] Was the warrant directed to a *class of officers* which included you?
- [ ] Did you observe *jurisdictional* limitations?
- [ ] Did you restrict service to proper *day/night* limits?
- [ ] Did you serve the warrant "forthwith," within the statutory *time limits?*
- [ ] Did you comply with *"knock-notice"* statutes or enter to prevent the immediate destruction of evidence or a threat to your safety?
- [ ] Did you limit the *scope* of your search to places where the warrant authorized, and to places where the objects might reasonably be found?
- [ ] Was any additional property seized after it *came into your view* while you were searching pursuant to the warrant?
- [ ] Did you leave a copy of the warrant and an inventory receipt with the occupant, or in a conspicuous place?
- [ ] Did you promptly file a *return* of the warrant with the issuing court, within prescribed time limits, listing only those seized items which were covered by the warrant?

- [ ] **IF A SEARCH-AND-SEIZURE ERROR OCCURRED, CAN THE CASE STILL BE SAVED?**
    - [ ] Were there *other justifications* for the search besides the one where the error occurred?
    - [ ] Was the search or seizure undertaken in objectively reasonable *good faith?*

- ☐ Did the passage of time and intervening events serve to *attenuate the taint* of the original error?
- ☐ Did you have an *independent source* of reaching the evidence, without really needing the tainted route?
- ☐ Would the evidence have been *inevitably discovered* in any event, even without the unlawful search or seizure?

NOTES

9

THE SUPPRESSION HEARING

I'm going to refer you to another of my books for a complete discussion of courtroom conduct and tactics. **COURTROOM SURVIVAL,** *The Officer's Guide To Better Testimony,* contains all of my suggestions on how to be a top-notch witness.

Again, however, I want to discuss briefly the special features of the courtroom review of your search-and-seizure activities. As I mentioned in Chapter 1, the defense attorney files a motion to suppress evidence, and a court hearing without a jury is scheduled to examine your search-and-seizure conduct for compliance with prevailing court decisions. This is the suppression hearing.

WHO HAS TO PROVE WHAT?

The burden of proof in the suppression hearing depends on just one thing: whether or not you had a warrant for the search or seizure that produced the contested evidence. If you had no warrant, the judge will start the hearing with a legal presumption that your search or seizure was unreasonable. That presumption puts the burden on the prosecution to prove that one or more of the exceptions fit your case.

If you *did* have a search warrant for the evidence, the judge will begin the hearing with a legal presumption that your search or seizure was reasonable. The defense then has the burden of proving a fatal defect in the affidavit or warrant, or of proving some error in your service of it.

As you see, there is a big difference between going into a suppression hearing with a warrant backing you up, and going in without one. This is just one more good reason why you should always try to obtain a warrant, if possible.

UNIQUE FEATURES OF THE HEARING

Because the focus of the suppression hearing is the reasonableness of your search or seizure—and not the guilt or innocence of the accused—there are a few differences between the rules for this hearing and the rules of trials.

Hearsay. With some exceptions, hearsay is not generally admissible at a trial. But statements which would be hearsay if offered as truth of facts in issue at a trial are *not* hearsay if they are offered in a suppression hearing to show the *basis* of your actions.

For example, a citizen comes up to you on the street and says: "I just saw Danny inside that building with a bunch of gold jewelry he stole. He has a furnace going and he's getting ready to melt it down." The citizen's statement to you would be inadmissible hearsay if you were repeating it at trial to prove that the jewelry was stolen, or that Danny had it, or that he was going to melt it down. But the statement is *not* hearsay if you repeat it at the suppression hearing in order to show your PC for believing a warrantless entry and search was necessary to prevent the imminent destruction of evidence.

Carelessly-uttered hearsay in the middle of a trial by jury can cause a mistrial to be declared. However, since there is no jury at the suppression hearing to be prejudiced by inadmissible hearsay, you don't need to worry about repeating hearsay at this hearing. Go ahead and tell the judge about any information that formed the basis for your action—even if it's based on statements which would be hearsay at a trial.

Conclusions and Opinions. The same rule applies here. Conclusions and opinions are not usually admissible at trial, but if they contributed to your PC to conduct a warrantless entry, search, or seizure, they are admissible for proof of PC at the suppression hearing. Don't hesitate to offer them.

For example, you're patrolling near a closed car lot one night when you see that the driveway chain is in pieces on the ground. Checking further, you see a car with the driver's door open and someone's legs sticking out. When you look in, you see a man holding a group of wires which are dangling from beneath the dashboard. You order him out and pat him down for weapons, and you find bolt cutters which are later matched to the bite marks on the cut driveway chain. Although you wouldn't be able to say, at the jury trial, "I thought he was trying to hot wire the car and steal it," you *can* offer this conclusion at the suppression hearing as part of your PC for frisking the suspect.

Understatement. I've had a number of suppression hearings at which officers tended to understate their probable cause, telling me later (after losing the hearing) that there were *other* things they took into consideration, but they didn't feel it was necessary to bring out everything, because they thought the facts they testified to would be quite sufficient to establish PC. They were surprised to learn that the judge had a different opinion.

You cannot overstate your PC. When you're explaining a warrantless entry, search or seizure, you should testify to every fact and observation, and the conclusions you drew, and omit no detail. One little "unimportant" fact could be just enough to tip the PC scales in your favor. Don't just concentrate on the major, obvious facts and leave out the smaller details— small details can add up. If there's any question in the judge's mind about the reasonableness of your conduct, he'll resolve it in the defendant's favor. Unless the prosecutor has advised you of a tactical reason for not mentioning some particular item, you should shoot all the PC ammunition you're carrying. Don't save anything back.

Debriefing. Win or lose (but especially if you lose), you should try to talk to the prosecutor after the hearing to find out what you did right, and what you did wrong, both in the field and in the courtroom. As I've said before, 4th Amendment law varies widely and changes frequently. A post-hearing debriefing with the prosecutor is one good way for you to keep up on the latest local interpretations of search-and-seizure law. It is also the very best way to learn about possible errors in your field conduct and in your testimony, and how to prevent them next time.

YOUR HARDEST JOB

Learning the rules on search and seizure isn't especially difficult—it just takes a little study time, a little research, and maybe some discussion with a local authority. *Applying* the rules is a little more difficult, because it requires you to judge new sets of facts as you encounter them, and to reason as you consider what you should do. Application of the rules also often requires that you exercise an unnatural degree of patience in developing probable cause, or abandoning a direct approach in order to obtain a search warrant. But if you have enough motivation and self-discipline, you can master the proper application of search-and-seizure law.

The *hardest* job for law enforcement officers is *changing* the rules on search and seizure. Short of a Constitutional amendment to put the exclusionary rule out of its misery, I don't know of any way to change the rules on search and seizure except through education. The hardest job you have in the search-and-seizure field is finding ways to educate attorneys and judges to those realities of police work which are either practically incompatible or completely irreconcilable with some of the current interpretations of 4th Amendment requirements.

One of the places where you have the opportunity to dispense some of this badly-needed education is at the suppression hearing. You have a chance to give thorough explanations of why you do your job the way you do, and why any other prudent officer would do exactly the same thing.

Here's an example from my personal experience. During a recent hearing on a defense motion to suppress evidence seized in the course of a carstop, it was established that the officer initially stopped the car for running a red light. Eventually, as a result of PC which the officer developed step-by-step after contacting the driver, the officer made a good arrest for possession of cocaine for sale, seizing 22 ounces of the drug.

At the suppression hearing, the defense lawyer soon saw that the post-carstop PC was solid, and so he resorted to an attack on the stop itself, trying to lay the foundation for a ruling that the officer had used the traffic violation as a *pretext* for contacting the driver. Since the officer had issued a citation for the red light violation, the defense attack focused on the *timing* of the carstop:

> Q: (By defense attorney) You said the light Mr. Sanchez ran was at 4th and Main, is that right, Officer?
> A: That's right.
> Q: And the carstop itself took place at about 2300 N. Main?
> A: Yes, sir.
> Q: Officer, what is the approximate distance you followed Mr. Sanchez from the place where he allegedly ran the light to the point where the stop was effected?
> A: That's approximately 1½ miles.
> Q: Thank you, Officer. Thank you very much.

This officer correctly confined each answer to the scope of the question he had been asked, so on the surface, to the attorney or judge who hadn't been educated, it might begin to appear that the officer followed Sanchez a suspiciously-long distance before making the stop. This could suggest that the officer was looking for something better than a red-light violation, and when he saw nothing, decided to go ahead and stop the car for a traffic violation occurring 1½ miles back: a pretext.

Having been a cop myself, I knew that there are several good reasons why a stop might well be delayed for 1½ miles. And having worked with this particular officer before, I knew that he would come through with some good explanations for this delay, given a chance. So, on redirect, I gave him a chance:

> Q: *(By prosecutor) Officer, was there any reason why you didn't stop Mr. Sanchez as soon as you saw the violation, in the vicinity of 400 N. Main?*
> A: *Yes, sir. In fact, there were . . . 4 reasons why I didn't stop him right away.*
> Q: *What was the first?*
> A: *We have an average of 35 officers who have to share 1 radio frequency at any given time, plus, there's 2 fire engine companies and 3 ambulances on the same net. What this means is that you can't get on the air to call in your carstop the instant you see the violation—you have to wait for an opening. That was one of the problems in this particular case. As I recall, the radio traffic was pretty heavy that evening.*
> Q: *Do you have a policy of calling in your car-stop* **before** *you turn on your overhead lights?*
> A: *Yes, sir.*
> Q: *Why is that?*
> A: *We call in the location of the stop and the license number of the car we're stopping so that if anything happens to us, the dispatcher will know where we are and will have a vehicle description and plate number to broadcast for other officers to check on.*

We also have to let the dispatcher know that we're occupied, so she won't try to send us on a call in the middle of our carstop. If you don't call this information in **before** *you turn on your overheads to stop the car, it's possible the guy will pull over immediately and jump out and make it back to your car while you're still trying to get on the air, and then your attention is split between the radio and some guy yelling through your window, and you're still sitting there in your car, at a disadvantage if he decides to pull something. Or, as soon as he sees your overheads, he starts to split, and you get into a high-speed pursuit and can't even get on the air to tell the dispatcher and other units about it. This is why we have a policy of getting the stop called in* **before** *we turn on the overhead lights.*

Q: *Alright. What was another reason why you didn't stop Mr. Sanchez right away?*

A: *As I was following him and waiting to get on the air, I recognized his car and license number from several previous contacts I'd had with Mr. Sanchez, when he had been wanted on outstanding arrest warrants. One of those times, he ran from me, and another time, we got into a fight. So before I stopped him for running the red light, I wanted to run a record check and see if he had any new warrants. If he did, I wanted to know about it before*

I tried stopping him, so I could request a back-up unit and wait til they were in place before pulling Mr. Sanchez over. I followed Mr. Sanchez for several more blocks while the warrant check was being run.

Q: *Did that warrant check show any outstanding warrants for Mr. Sanchez?*
A: *No, sir.*
Q: *And did you then pull him over right away?*
A: *No, sir.*
Q: *Why not?*
A: *It was a bad area for a carstop.*
Q: *Why was that?*
A: *For one thing, the street is narrow there and there were cars parked along the curb, which meant we would have had to stop in a traffic lane, and this would have backed up traffic and created a possible hazard for people trying to go around us. For another thing, there are a lot of driveways, sidestreets, alleys, and commercial buildings along both sides of Main from the 400 block to about 1900 North. If you stop a car in an area like that, you're giving the driver a lot of places to flee to, if he has a reason to flee that you don't know about, and you're making it tougher to contain him or to find him. On the other hand, a little ways further north, starting at about 2000 N. Main, there's a block wall fence running all along the east side and an open field all along the west side. And*

there's no curb parking there, and the road is wider. So a stop there causes less of a traffic problem, and it practically eliminates any escape routes or cover for a fleeing suspect. That's why I delayed my stop a little longer after being told that there were no warrants out on Mr. Sanchez.

Q: Why didn't you pull him over in the 2000 block of N. Main, instead of waiting to the 2300 block?

A: I started calling in the stop as soon as I could see we were both clear of the intersection of 20th and Main, which is a busy intersection that time of the evening. When you call in your stop, depending on the speed of the car and the distance between you, you have to try to project how far it's going to take the driver to respond and yield, and you call your stop a block or two in advance. In other words, if you call in when you hit the 2000 block and tell the dispatcher you're making a stop **there**, she has you down at 2000 N. Main. But you hit your overheads and it takes awhile for the guy to notice and react, and by the time he finally pulls over, you're up in the 2300 block, and now you've got to try to get back on the air and let the dispatcher know where you finally wound up. And in the meantime, maybe the driver is on his way back to see you, and you don't want to get caught sitting in your car where you can't take precautions for your own safety. All of these various things, which are fairly typical considerations on a carstop of this nature—that's what accounted for this approximately 1½ mile delay, or distance, between the location of the violation and the location where Mr. Sanchez finally stopped his car.

Q: Thank you, Officer. No further questions.

You see? This cop did a great job of educating a judge and a skeptical attorney to some of the practical considerations of field work that aren't that obvious to courtroom personnel. (Mr. Sanchez, I'm happy to report, lost his suppression motion, lost his appeal, lost his trial, and went off to state prison to rue the day he ran a red light in front of G.L. Rogers).

Remember that standard problems and procedures you encounter everyday—things that are just "routine" to a working officer—are often well-kept secrets from the very people who review your conduct for reasonableness. Don't assume that because something is obvious to you, or is an old, established police custom, the judge and the lawyers must be aware of it. Chances are, they're not. If the particular procedure has something to do with explaining and justifying your actions, it's your job to educate court officials to it. There's no one else to do it. And the sooner the courts learn about some of the dangers and necessities of law enforcement work, the sooner court rulings can begin to take proper account of reality.

DOING THE BEST YOU CAN

Let's not part company with any misunderstandings. I can't guarantee you that if you learn and follow all the accepted search-and-seizure rules, you will always win every suppression hearing and every case. You won't. What you *will* do is increase your odds of winning far more frequently than you would without this knowledge. But it is still possible that every now and then, you may do everything "by the book," flawlessly, and *still* lose the evidence in a suppression hearing.

Why? For one thing, courts sometimes alter the rules *retroactively,* and you're stuck with what you did under the old rules. For another thing, a judge may sometimes decide to believe the defendant and his carload of witnesses over the testimony of an outnumbered officer.

And as you already know (or will soon find out), the people over in the courthouse who interpret the law and pass judgment on your conduct are human beings, too. They're no more infallible than you are. They also make mistakes. So even though you may have made a perfectly legal, perfectly reasonable search or seizure, you may find in an occasional case that the court makes a perfectly unreasonable ruling.

For example, in *Paschal v. State,* a radio broadcast described an armed robbery vehicle, but gave no further details. An alert officer saw the car almost immediately, pulled it over, searched, and found evidence of the crime. The Alabama court suppressed the evidence, ruling that the *radio broadcast did not give the officer any PC for a warrantless search!*

In *US v. Dunbar,* a state trooper saw that a driver was apparently lost at a confusing intersection. He stopped to give directions and saw bombs and other explosives in the car, which resulted in a seizure and a federal charge of illegal possession and transportation of explosive devices. The federal court in Connecticut suppressed the evidence, ruling that *the trooper had no PC to contact the driver to render assistance, so the items which were then in plain view in a fleeting automobile could not be admitted!*

A federal judge in Massachusetts reversed a murder conviction in *US v. Charest* because he didn't think the affidavit for the search warrant, issued 16 days after the murder, established a probability of finding the murder weapon at the defendant's house (which is exactly where officers found it). Said the court: "Common sense tells us it is unlikely that a murderer would hide, in his own home, a gun used to shoot someone. The first thing he would do is get rid of the gun." (This judge obviously isn't in touch with the facts of the criminal mentality; it doesn't even appear that he was in touch with the facts of the case.)

And for a final example of injudicious adjudication, there was the trial judge in Kentucky who ruled that a blood sample taken from a dead driver's body for alcohol analysis *violated the decedent's rights against unconstitutional search and seizure!* (This decision was promptly reversed by an embarrassed Kentucky Supreme Court.)

I didn't put these ludicrous examples at the end here to discourage you. These decisions are *extreme* and *isolated* cases of exceptionally poor judgment. I just wanted you to keep in mind that even the most carefully-constructed case can sometimes come apart, through no fault of yours, due to circumstances completely beyond your control. The odds, however, are greatly in your favor that your adherence to proper search-and-seizure procedure will be appropriately recognized and will almost always contribute to the successful prosecution of the case. That's the best we can hope for.

And no matter which way the lawyers and the judges adjudge your field conduct at the end of the suppression hearing, you still have to judge yourself. Believe me, there is a huge difference between walking out of the courthouse with the feeling that the judge was right and you were wrong, and walking out with the confidence that *despite* a retroactive change, or *despite* being outnumbered by a carload of liars, or *despite* having to appear before a disappointing judge, you did the best thing you could do at the time, and *you* can live with your actions. When you've done the best you can, you've done *all* you can. ☐

Order Today!
OUR MOST POPULAR CRIMINAL JUSTICE TITLES...

California Criminal Law $19.95
Community Relations Concepts $24.95
Courtroom Survival $14.95
Officer's Guide to Better Testimony
Criminal Interrogation $19.95
Laws and Tactics
Fingerprint Science $18.95
How to Roll, Classify, File and Use Fingerprints
The Officer Survival Manual $15.95
The *New* Police Report Manual $14.95
PC 832 Concepts II $18.95
Police Unarmed Defense Tactics $9.95
Practical Criminal Investigation $29.95
Principles of Amer. Law Enf. & Crim. Justice $34.95
The Search and Seizure Handbook $15.95
Traffic Investigation and Enforcement $21.95
Understanding Street Gangs $19.95

Mail to:
CUSTOM PUBLISHING COMPANY
P.O. Box 604 Sonora, CA 95370
1-800-223-4838 *orders only*
(In California call (209) 532-5050)
Please enclose payment or departmental purchase order.

Card # ____ - ____ - ____ - ____   Visa/MC (circle one)

Exp. Date ____/____   Telephone(___) _____

Signature _____
(Signature required for all charge cards purchases)
Address _____

City _____ St ____ Zip _____

SALES TAX: California residents add applicable sales tax.
We Pay Shipping
Order Today!